COMPASSION IN DYING DISCARD

Stories of
Dignity and Choice

Edited by
BARBARA COOMBS LEE

Foreword by
BARBARA ROBERTS

NEWSAGE PRESS
TROUTDALE, OREGON

Compassion in Dying:
Stories of Dignity and Choice
Copyright © 2003 Barbara Coombs Lee
ISBN 0-939165-49-X

NewSage Press
PO Box 607
Troutdale, OR 97060-0607
503-695-2211

website: www.newsagepress.com
email: info@newsagepress.com

Cover and Book Design by Sherry Wachter
Printed in the United States on recycled paper
Distributed in the United States and Canada by Publishers Group West

Library of Congress Cataloging-in-Publication Data

Compassion in dying : stories of dignity and hope / edited by Barbara Coombs Lee ; foreword by Barbara Roberts.
p. cm.
Includes bibliographical references and index.
ISBN 0-939165-49-X
1. Palliative treatment. 2. Palliative treatment—Anecdotes. 3.Dying. 4. Terminal care. 5. Terminal care—Anecdotes. 6. Terminal care—Law and legislation—Oregon. 7. Right to die—Law and legislation—Oregon. 8. Terminally ill—Legal status, laws, etc.—Oregon. I. Lee, Barbara Coombs, 1947-
362.17'5—dc22

2003017627

1 2 3 4 5 6 7 8 9

Dedication

For the individuals who, over ten years since Compassion in Dying began, have asked us to accompany them on their end-of-life journeys. They have taught us everything we know about courage, hope, and dignity, and how to be of help to the terminally ill and their loved ones.

Acknowledgments

This book reflects community—the Compassion community, where dedicated individuals combine their skills to serve patients and create a movement. Even though it is impossible to recognize everyone who helped make this book possible it would be a shame not to recognize at least a few.

Maureen Michelson of NewSage Press provided the inspiration and the conviction that it could be done. Her editorial guidance helped us complete this project in fewer than twelve months. Claire Simons gave her impressive energies to the task of gathering the stories from a variety of sources. Her attention to detail and commitment to the project have been invaluable. Barbara Roberts led the way with her own book, *Death Without Denial, Grief Without Apology,* and showed us how to open our hearts in print.

The talented book designer, Sherry Wachter, created this handsome volume and beautiful book cover. Kate Hummel gathered final approvals from participants in the book, and Tracy Smith of NewSage Press proofed the final pages. Scores of others pitched in with their support and assistance as deadlines loomed.

We owe a special acknowledgment to all who agreed to participate in this book, sharing their thoughts and feelings openly. Without you this book would not have been possible.

Judith Fleming is the spark that ignited Compassion of Oregon and continues to spread its light in the community. George Eighmey, his board of directors, his medical advisor, and his impressive team of volunteers serve Oregon tirelessly and have turned its aid in dying law into a realistic model for the nation. Helen Beum keeps a steady, even hand on volunteer training, continuing education, and oversight of each case.

Numerous charitable foundations and thousands of individual contributors support the work of Compassion so we can serve the public without charge and create the hope and dignity reflected in these stories. To everyone, family and friends, who have sustained the energetic, year-long writing process and encouraged us during times of stress and intensity, we express our sincere gratitude.

Contents

Foreword

BARBARA ROBERTS
Oregon Governor, 1991 - 1995

*L*ife is a terminal condition. Death will come to each of us. Yet, if there is anything Americans wish to avoid discussing, find more threatening to face, and routinely skip making preparations for, it is our own inevitable death.

I have come to understand that dying is more difficult in a culture of denial. Grieving is more painful and lonely in a society of silence.

As a native Oregonian and a former governor, I am frequently asked by nonresidents how Oregon's Death with Dignity Law ever came to pass. Let me answer with a short history lesson on Oregon's aid in dying law.

The law came to the Oregon ballot as a citizen sponsored initiative in November 1994. The measure passed on a squeaker vote—winning by a 51 percent margin. A court challenge by the National Right to Life Committee kept the law from going into effect. That lawsuit's failure put the law back in the legislature's hands. The 1997 legislative session spent months arguing over the details of implementation, looking for improved legal and medical safeguards, and continually implying that Oregon voters did not know what they were doing when they passed that landmark law. So, in its political wisdom, unable to find improvements, the 1997 legislature placed a repeal of the original Act on the

November ballot. This time the voters made their message very clear—
the voters approved the law with a 60 percent margin.

After two well-funded, controversial statewide campaigns, Oregon
voters became the best informed Americans on the subjects of dying,
pain medication, heroic medical procedures, advance directives, and
hospice care. Every television-viewing evening brought our citizens the
pro and con positions on the ballot measure. Ad after ad detailed opinions on dying. Strong opinions filled letters-to-the-editor sections, editorial columns, front pages, and radio airwaves. Family and friends discussed the proposal over dinner, at bowling alleys, at hair salons, in
classrooms, and churches and synagogues. Dying was out of the closet
in Oregon.

But there is another important piece of the story—an earlier history. Dating back to the 1980s, a small number of Oregonians were
asking questions about the dying process. Why should pain medications be withheld or limited for dying patients? Did advance directives and living wills have the force of law? As medical science
advanced and the means to keep patients alive with machines grew
more common, when did patients and families have the right to say,
"Enough"? Many senior citizens expressed a greater fear of nursing
homes and hospitals than actually dying. One of the most pressing
questions became, "Doesn't how we die matter as much as how
we live?"

My late husband, State Senator Frank Roberts, was one of those rais-
ing the questions. During his long legislative career he championed the
rights of individuals to have options on end-of-life matters. He sponsored many bills, a number of which passed, that gave Oregonians, for

example, the right to appoint a person to make health care decisions for them if they were unable to do so themselves. One bill assured a person's right to stop receiving extraordinary measures to keep him or her alive, including life support systems. On several occasions, Frank sponsored laws to allow terminal patients to hasten their death under carefully controlled conditions. In the political climate of the legislative process, those more controversial laws never left committee.

So why did Frank introduce all this legislation? He did so because he passionately and compassionately believed adults had the knowledge, ability, wisdom—and the right—to decide their own fate. And perhaps, looking back, he may have had some premonition of what was to come for him at the end of his own life. Frank died a prolonged and difficult cancer death. In the last weeks of his life he spoke often and wistfully of his proposed aid in dying legislation. But he did not live to see the Oregon measure reach the ballot or to celebrate the passage of Oregon's Death with Dignity Act in 1994.

In the final months of Frank's life, when I was Governor of Oregon and he was still serving as a State Senator, we spoke openly and publicly about his impending death. I believe our openness encouraged greater public discussion among all Oregonians about death and dying. I know for certain, if Frank were alive today, he would be proud to know his progressive legislation moved forward due to the efforts of this state's citizens and the initiative process. He would be comforted knowing the law has been rarely used and has worked without negative complications for the dying. He would applaud the work of Compassion in Dying. And he would not be surprised to find that many qualified terminal patients with the prescription in their refrigerator chose not to use it. Frank would fully understand the Oregonians who simply want the option and find comfort that the choice is available to them.

When Frank died at home in the Governor's residence on October 31, 1993, he had faced a terminal diagnosis for a year. He had been under hospice care for six months. In the last weeks of his illness he became the "poster child" for his right-to-die legislation. He was bed-ridden, suffered a stroke, was no longer able to eat, needed constant pain medication, and expressed his readiness to die. I did not want Frank to die—he was my love, my confidant, my friend. But, at that point, I couldn't wish for him to live any longer. Now, Oregon patients in a similar situation have a choice available to them. That was all Frank ever wanted for himself and others—choice.

In Oregon, even those who voted against the Death with Dignity Act and those who may still oppose it, can recognize clearly that Oregon has used the law sparingly with total adherence to the letter and the spirit of the Act. Plus, the word "dignity" has been the hallmark of this ground-breaking law. Oregon's law was carefully drafted with the safeguards and guidelines in the legal language that assured our citizens that such precautions would prevent abuse and misuse. Without those legal protections, Oregon voters never would have passed the measure.

I believe if the aid in dying law were on the ballot in Oregon in 2003, it would pass by 70 percent or more. And one of the strongest reasons for that growing support is the Compassion in Dying organization. Compassion has become the steward of our unique law. Since the law's implementation in 1997, Compassion has been the leading advocate and support organization for patients, families, physicians, and the law. Those who predicted a Kevorkian-like sideshow in Oregon have been silenced, one by one, as the law has been applied with care and compassion.

In the ten years since Frank's difficult death, I have learned much about the dying process in Oregon and America. I served on both the Oregon Hospice Association board of directors and the National Hospice Advisory Board. I am currently on the Advisory Board for Oregon Compassion in Dying. I spent part of a year as a volunteer in an AIDS hospice. Since the publication of my first book, *Death Without Denial, Grief Without Apology* (NewSage Press 2002) I have heard many personal stories of death and grief from individuals across the nation. I believe that which we can talk about we can make better.

I know this about Oregon: We lead the nation in the number of terminally ill patients enrolled in hospice. Oregon is one of the leaders in the use of morphine to treat pain for dying patients. We have more people die at home and fewer citizens die in intensive care units than anywhere in the nation. We are considered a model state in end-of-life care. Oregon's Death with Dignity Act has made the dying process an open and acceptable topic in Oregon communities and families. As we have ended the silence, progress has followed.

I am grateful to Oregon citizens for their vision and courage and compassion in caring so deeply about their fellow citizens. I hold those at Compassion in Dying in high regard for their on-going dedication and their ability to face, first-hand, the terminally ill and to hold the hands and the hearts of those facing death.

A law is only as good as those who implement that law, and this nation should feel grateful to Oregon's voters and to Compassion in

Dying for demonstrating the courage and wisdom to know when to acknowledge gently, "Enough."

Oregon has become the role model for death with dignity. We have drafted the blueprint for others to follow. In a culture of medical miracles and scientific expansion, we must not lose sight of the need to accept death as a realistic part of the life cycle.

Some are determined to take a sledgehammer to Oregon's law. For those who disagree with the choice Oregon has made, I say this: "I hope millions of Americans will read this extraordinary volume that captures the gentle wisdom of Oregon's law and cites the brave choices made by Oregonians who used our Death with Dignity Act and those who have been its supporters." These are stories of caring, courage, and compassion. They are stories of lives well lived and deaths well chosen. They are the stories that represent the benchmarks for personal decision-making in life's final scene.

I hope you will read this book with an open mind. If you do so, you will understand more fully the remarkable choice Oregon voters have made. You will see more clearly the option of a gentle exit. You will be able to embrace the strength and courage of the terminally ill and their loved ones.

Oregon's law is not rooted in controversy. It is grounded in love and caring. To some it is an experimental law. To others it is the answer to a prayer. However you react to Oregon's legal choice for its terminally ill citizens, I hope you will withhold judgment until you have read the moving and honest stories that fill the pages of this unique book. *Compassion in Dying* offers you a front row seat to caring scenes of death bravely shared by family and loved ones.

A Death of One's Own

While I did not understand its importance at the time, a lesson from one of my first patients greatly influenced the work that eventually became my calling. My first job after nursing school was as charge nurse on a ward of a busy metropolitan hospital. There I met Richard, two years younger than I, and dying of leukemia. His parents were heartbroken and estranged from their son. They rarely entered his hospital room, instead spending days and nights in the solarium at the end of the hall.

One day Richard asked me how he would die and I answered him honestly. "You will probably start bleeding too rapidly to replace the blood loss with transfusions. Death will be painless and peaceful." I also shared with Richard my hope that he and his parents would reconcile before that happened. At that time, I felt *entitled* to nudge him toward reconciliation. Twice I raised the subject; then Richard firmly put me in my place. "Oh, no. Not you, too," he said. "Everyone has their own agenda for me. But this is *my* death and I'll do it my own way."

Richard was right. I had tried to impose my own desires and set him on a course that felt right to me. Instead of helping him ask questions, I was trying to give answers. This was the beginning of my supreme respect for the beliefs, values, and preferences of any person who is close to death.

The realization that respect for the dying had a political component came many years later. As a lawyer, I staffed the Oregon Senate committee through which Senator Frank Roberts, a revered statesman, wanted to introduce a bill to allow physician aid in dying. The Senator had terminal cancer, the stature of a long and distinguished career, and the advantage of being married to the Governor. But even with all this prestige and experience, he could not get a fair hearing for his bill.

So the note in my church bulletin about a group organizing to place an aid in dying bill on the statewide ballot caught my attention. That was 1993. I responded and events fell into place so exactly that my work at Compassion in Dying Federation now feels like a call. It is the work for which my life prepared me.

The stories in this collection come from individuals who have turned to Compassion for hope, dignity, and choice in their process of dying. In particular the featured individuals in this book wanted the option of aid in dying, legal under Oregon's Death with Dignity Act. Some used the prescribed medication to hasten death, while others died from natural causes. However, they all derived great comfort from knowing they had achieved choice and control at the end-of-life.

I became friends and political allies with some of these remarkable individuals as we worked together to establish and maintain the law in Oregon. I greatly admired Penny Schleuter as she stood up to the Oregon legislature and implored lawmakers to keep their promise not to repeal the aid in dying law. She did so in spite of worsening pain and weakness as her ovarian cancer progressed rapidly. Penny died long before our battle was over, but others have selflessly followed her. They remind me of soldiers on a battlefield who pick up the staff when a flag-bearer falls. Kate Cheney courageously offered her story to the press in order to ease the process for others. Jim Romney and Richard Holmes joined the legal fight against federal government intervention, becoming both petitioners and spokesmen for the cause. Now they, too, have passed on. But other decent, brave, and forthright individuals will follow them. Individuals who, in the words of Jim Romney "stand tall" to their dying day for the values they hold dear. These are the same values America holds dear: Liberty—Independence—Responsibility—Faith.

These courageous individuals, and their families and friends have shared their thoughts and feelings openly in hopes of furthering a national dialogue. The stories from those who have died are drawn from interviews, tapes, and memories of their final gatherings, and their own writings. Families and friends agreed to be interviewed or to write about their thoughts, complex emotions, convictions, and final good-byes with loved ones. We also included stories from Compassion volunteers and religious leaders who work with individuals considering assisted dying.

These stories hold great wisdom from those who precede us in death. They are the pioneers—forging the way in a social movement committed to relieving human suffering and enhancing choice at the end of life. One important lesson we at Compassion have learned is that a passion about the manner of dying often reflects an equal and lifelong passion about joyful and richly textured living. Coming to terms with death brings our values into bold relief. As Epicurus observed centuries ago, "The art of living well and dying well are one."

The stories in this book reflect attitudes and values shared by many Americans. These values shape Compassion's advocacy for autonomy and self-determination. They provide the conviction and the form behind that advocacy. They demonstrate the beneficial results of that advocacy.

Since 1993 Compassion in Dying has promoted individual autonomy for people confronting the end of their lives. People have momentous decisions to make when dying and our job is to inform and support their decisions. The rich stories in this book reveal the complexities of end-of-life issues and the human need to affirm deeply held values. By sharing these stories we hope to help others confronting similar situations and to help society understand how the issues of a national debate play out in the lives of people who might be their neighbors, their friends, their role models.

The staff and volunteers at Compassion have served as knowledgeable resources and steadfast allies to thousands of terminally ill individuals. We have witnessed their anguish, shared their frustration, and rejoiced at their victories over difficult circumstances. We have defended their rights in Oregon acquired with passage of a law legalizing aid in dying and asserted the same rights for patients in other states.

Court battles postponed Oregon's legal framework until October 1997. By that time Compassion already had more than four years' experience counseling patients throughout the nation about aid in dying. Compassion came to Oregon prepared with a proven model and accumulated expertise. Following a protocol of careful screening, supportive counseling, and interdisciplinary planning, Compassion volunteers have attended approximately three quarters of Oregon's assisted dying cases. Our medical advisor, a retired oncologist, has contributed countless hours to guide hundreds of physicians through elaborate legal responsibilities. Generous volunteers have advocated for pain treatment, counseled families, educated hospice staff, and served as loyal and trusted companions on countless end-of-life journeys. Through many acts of kindness, diligence, and skill, Oregon rose to the top of the nation in end-of-life care and became the exemplar of choice, integrated into excellent comfort care.

In the first five years of the law's use 198 Oregonians completed the eligibility process for assisted dying. Of those, 129 took the medication to die. But thousands of other Oregonians were comforted knowing they had the option of hastening death if trapped in an unbearable situation. With about 30,000 Oregonians dying each year, it is clear only a very small percentage use medication under the law to hasten their death. But the psychological impact of the law has empowered patients and changed the dynamics of end-of-life care forever throughout the state. One of the most heartening results of Oregon's assisted dying law is how it has prompted enormous improvement in the quality of care for dying patients.

As this book goes to press August 2003, U.S. Attorney General John Ashcroft is acting on his personal belief that the Oregon law on physician aid in dying is morally wrong. He is using his position as the nation's chief law enforcement officer to threaten doctors who participate in the law with federal prosecution for drug diversion and abuse.

Ashcroft and others have made numerous attempts to reverse Oregon's Death with Dignity Act, the first law in the nation to legalize aid in dying. Oregonians voted twice, in 1994 and 1997, to allow mentally competent, terminally ill, adult residents to request from their attending physicians medication they could take at a time and place of their choosing to hasten death. (I list the parameters of this law on page 132.) To date, neither Ashcroft nor right-to-life activists nor opponents in Congress have succeeded, but their challenges continue.

Americans have a passion for personal liberty. We like to make our own choices. We want the law to protect our liberties. But the law often thwarts the liberty of the terminally ill. If a person abhors the prospect of a prolonged dying process, intolerable suffering, and relentless bodily disintegration, the law in most states bars the legal, open, and honest hastening of death. Instead of a law like Oregon's delineating guidelines, safeguards, and oversight to provide choice and prevent abuse, the terminally ill who consider hastening their deaths in other states face two cardinal rules: (1) Keep it Secret and (2) Die Alone.

It is offensive to most Americans that the government imposes such rules. Perhaps never in the course of life is liberty more cherished than when faced with hard choices about life and death. Liberty is essential to a sense of authentic living, and a democratic nation cannot protect its citizens from hard choices by robbing them of liberty.

Americans value responsibility for others, especially caring for family. Yet across the nation the many individuals who wish to hasten their deaths tell their families to leave the bedside to avoid the risk of criminal prosecution. A statement to the U.S. Supreme Court from a woman named Kay Beck says, "On November 11, 1991, I helped my husband Jack end his life. To classify me as a criminal because I refused to leave my husband's side at this time of greatest loss I find unconscionable. We must change this law…or be prepared to put people like me in jail."

The alternative to peaceful, legal aid in dying is often tragic. Compassion received a letter from a daughter whose father, dying of cancer, despaired of finding a doctor willing to test the law in his state and write a prescription for medication to hasten death. Instead, he went to his barn and shot himself. His daughter wrote:

> My father was a man who always "took care" of things—as a child helping put food on the table by hunting and fishing during the Depression, as a soldier in the army, as a husband, father, and carpenter. Nothing ever broke at our house because of his preventive maintenance. He logically thought out potential problems and prepared for them. He would quietly take control and resolve the situation. His final act was no different. He had thoroughly thought out his situation, determined his best course of action, and then, in his usual efficient, tidy manner, completed the task.
>
> I have come to accept this as his last way of caring for us— especially me, as he knew I was the one who would have provided an alternative method. Life was not good. It was time to go. I feel no guilt for trying to help my father and hold no blame for what he did. I hope that by talking about this to whomever will listen, his violent death will in some small way help find a more gentle way.

Such tragedies are completely preventable. Since 1998 Compassion has recorded fifty-nine potential violent suicides prevented in Oregon by enabling a legal and peaceful choice. Most of these individuals died naturally of their illness. Only twenty took medication to hasten their death.

Experience in Oregon teaches us that the legal option of aid in dying prevents violent suicides, promotes excellent end-of-life care, prompts physicians to treat dying patients more attentively, and increases use of hospice. The option of aid in dying brings comfort, peace, and hope to many thousands who never actually exercise a choice under the law.

Depriving people of this hope, this comfort, this assurance of a peaceful death, is wrong.

In addition to political opponents, there are those who champion the view that yearning for death is always pathologic and assisting a terminally ill individual to hasten the moment of death is morally wrong. This also includes those who hold fast to the redemptive power of suffering as the path to everlasting life in the presence of God. The difference between these perspectives arises from fundamentally different attitudes toward life, death, and divine power.

At Compassion we honor whatever a person might sense as transcendent or divine. Identified as religion, spirituality, interconnectedness, mystery or oneness, most Americans cherish their faith and relationship with a sacred and unknowable essence. This value merges with individuality to make how we die a very personal religious decision. Quoting the Philosophers Brief in Compassion's U.S. Supreme Court aid in dying cases *Vacco v. Quill* and *Washington v. Glucksberg:* "Most of us see death—whatever we think will follow it—as the final act of life's drama, and we want that last act to reflect our own convictions, those we have tried to live by, not the convictions of others forced on us in our most vulnerable moment."

Facing death with our senses intact, sharing farewells and closure with family, exiting with courage and grace can have deep spiritual meaning for those whose relationship with the Divine embraces those values. For them, affirming these values affirms the sanctity of the gift of life.

Americans pride themselves on a sense of fairness. But it is not fair that individuals have to endure prolonged dying and purposeless suffering against their will. They should not have the sweetness of their lives and the fond parting of their deaths stolen by the fear of an agonized ending. People should be able to choose a peaceful and humane death that comports with their values, beliefs, and concepts of integrity and right living. They should not have to hide their hopes for a gentle death, nor should they be forced to act alone, covertly, violently, or prematurely in order to protect family, friends, and physicians from prosecution.

Facing a terminal illness raises profound questions. But a government that answers them for its citizens is paternalistic and coercive. In a free, pluralistic society it is the responsibility of citizens to make these most central, life-defining judgments about their own lives. Of course patients face hard choices. The fact that these choices are difficult and personal is all the greater reason for the individual to make them and not the government. As Hubert Humphrey once said, "There are not enough jails, not enough policemen, not enough courts to enforce a law that is not supported by the people." The absence in most states of a fair and legal framework strikes me as a supreme injustice.

The stories in *Compassion in Dying* move the discussion of choice in dying beyond polarized political rhetoric. The details of these lives and deaths call us back to the humanity of dying and every individual's need for compassion, nonjudgmental listening, and respect. Regardless of one's political and personal beliefs on aid in dying, we can all learn from these personal stories of courage and care in the face of humankind's ultimate challenge—to accept our mortality with grace and serenity.

—BARBARA COOMBS LEE
AUGUST 2003

JIM ROMNEY

*Just knowing that this law is
an available option is very liberating
for a person with my condition...
I may go out and catch a chinook salmon
on the Columbia tomorrow.*

JIM ROMNEY

One

Jim Romney

Jim Romney loved life and always lived it to the fullest. Above all, he loved children: his own family as well as all the teenagers he influenced during his years as a high school educator and principal at Rainier High School.

In 2002, Jim's former students sent glowing notes of appreciation, reflecting a profound admiration for Jim and what he gave to them. One student wrote, "Everyone goes through life hoping they'll make an impact on someone. We want you to know you've succeeded...you've made a huge impact on us. Thanks for everything." Another high school senior wrote, "I hope you'll make it to graduation. If not, you'll be in my heart and I'll be thinking of you throughout the ceremony. I'll never forget you."

Jim and Kathy Romney have four grown children, and three grandchildren. They have shared a love for the outdoors ever since their children were small. Now with families of their own, their children still camp and water-ski together. Jim also loved the thrill of challenging physical activity. A skydiver, Jim figured he had made more than 500 jumps. He used to snow ski, water ski, snowboard, fish, and golf. As a young man, Jim played semi-professional tennis.

However, in June 2001 the Romneys' active lives changed dramatically when Jim, 56, was diagnosed with amyotrophic lateral sclerosis (ALS), also called Lou Gehrig's disease. ALS gradually destroys the connection between nerves and muscles. Eventually the disease robs one of the ability to stand, speak, swallow, and breathe. Many people stricken with ALS describe the disease as "every day there's a little death."

Faced with his own mortality, Jim revisited his Mormon upbringing. He did not believe in the traditional Mormon philosophy although he lived the teachings. He was also a staunch Republican, and realized that his personal decision would conflict with his political party's public platform. Former Michigan Governor George Romney and Massachusetts Governor Mitt Romney are Jim's cousins. But Jim wanted the choice to die on his own terms and not be hooked up to machines. He told his four siblings, "My God would not want me to suffer." All of them supported Jim's decision, and three siblings who are devout Mormons responded, "This is not of scripture but we love you and support your decision."

Jim became eligible for the Oregon Death with Dignity Act, relieved that he had options. But less than a month later, in November 2001, Attorney General John Ashcroft attempted to nullify Oregon's law by threatening to convict physicians who prescribed lethal doses of medication.

Incensed, two days later Jim volunteered to become a plaintiff, along with Richard Holmes, in the lawsuit, *Oregon v. Ashcroft.* In his court declaration Jim stated, "I do not intend to live my final days without control over my daily life." Jim told a *New York Times* reporter, "I was devastated, totally shocked by Ashcroft's announcement. It set me back. It took away all my sense of liberty. Believe me, just knowing that this law is an available option is very liberating for a person with my condition, and they're trying to take it away from me." The state of Oregon immediately got a temporary restraining order to keep the law in place. In April 2002, a U.S. Federal Court judge ruled that the Ashcroft directive was without force or effect and physicians could continue to prescribe medication for aid in dying. Oregon's Death with Dignity Act was still in place. At a press conference announcing the court decision, Jim told a room full of reporters, "I feel so liberated today that I may go out and catch a Chinook salmon on the Columbia tomorrow."

After that, Jim received his prescribed medication and intended to use it if the ALS robbed him of all quality of life. "When the time comes, I plan to have a single malt Scotch and off we go," Jim quipped. He was also open to the possibility that he would die naturally. But no matter how it happened, Jim was sure of one thing: he wanted his wife, children, and puppy gathered around him when he died.

Jim Romney's wife, Kathy, joined him in the interview for this book in February 2003. Kathy is a part-time teacher as well as Jim's primary caregiver. Jim died three months after this final interview.

※

JIM: Fourth of July in the summer of 2000, I was fishing with my nephew at Diamond Lake. It was cold in the morning, and I noticed my right hand was numb. I warmed up and it seemed better, but then continued to be numb. So I thought maybe I had a pinched nerve and went to the doctor. He referred me on to the neurologist, and for the next six to eight months they continued to take various tests. Finally, in June 2001, they diagnosed me with ALS.

By then I sensed what was coming, so I was already doing a lot of research about the disease. I had made the decision years ago that should I need to, I would hasten my own death because I think it's important that a person live and die with dignity. I went to the Hemlock Society and talked for some time to a man there. He said, "You can always put a bag of helium over your head."

I thought, *There's got to be a better way of going.* It didn't seem a very dignified way to go, with a bag over your head. Then he said I might want to talk with the people at Compassion in Dying, and I did. I went to the office of Compassion and met George Eighmey and asked how could they help me.

Not long after that we had the court case, and that was devastating because I thought, *Is my option gone? Do I have to go out in the back-yard and shoot myself?* Or I could go up in a plane one more time, just don't pull the cord; or fall off my fishing boat. But I don't want a violent death. That wouldn't be good for my family.

That fall, I went on a tour. I got my big truck and my camper, didn't take my boat—darn it, should have—and went to see every one of my four brothers and sisters; I drove to Las Vegas, Colorado, Salt Lake. I told them about the disease and that death with dignity is very important for me, and that I plan on getting medication within six months of dying. They were all supportive and accepting, mostly because I am who I am, and even though it's different than what the Mormon people believe, they all have been very supportive. They realize that it is my decision.

My sister Dawn died of pancreatic cancer at sixty-nine, just six months ago. She was very religious. My oldest sister is like me in her feelings about the Mormon philosophy. I have two brothers who are devout Mormons. They've both been bishops of their own wards. My oldest brother who is sixty-nine, he is back in Washington D.C. right now on a mission with his wife, and they have five kids, and all the boys went on missions. My other brother lives in Salt Lake and has five children. Two of his sons and a daughter are off on Mormon missions. Something I've really appreciated about my brothers and sisters is their focus on the family. I've always valued family. We've been to a couple of family reunions lately where all the kids were there and the grandkids. There are probably about fifty of us in the Romney family. I realize the importance of family, more recently than ever, because I take nothing for granted any more.

KATHY: I have never really known Jim not being active, playing tennis, lots of golf, lots of fishing. This in his spare time, of course, from a job that is so demanding—twelve-hour days being a high school principal or superintendent. We lived for three years in Port Orford on the Oregon Coast and that's when he became an avid fisherman. Then we moved to Roseburg and lived on the Umpqua River, the perfect place to pursue his fishing.

When Jim was diagnosed with ALS, it was almost unbelievable. All these sports, and working out almost every day at the gym, how could this happen to his muscles? That's the part that's been so difficult for both of us and for his family and friends, to see that happen.

Our family is very strong, and we were close before all this happened, but we've become much closer because of it. Our family, by being so close, has given all of us the strength to deal with what's happening to Jim. I think that without family it would be difficult for anyone.

JIM: My mother was the strongest woman I've ever known, except for Kathy. She never took a day off sick from work. She went to work every morning at 5:20, and every night we sat down to dinner at 6:00. My father died at fifty, obese and alcoholic; my mother was the strong person in the family. Even when I was young, she always said that if she was to be sick and tied up to a bunch of machines, not in control, "Give me the green pill." I had no idea what a green pill was, but I knew she would take it to hasten her own death. My bet is that's where my inner strength came from.

KATHY: It surprises me that a lot of my friends and family have said, "You're such a strong person and you're so calm about what's happening." I haven't always seen myself as a real strong person, but I think a lot of my strength has come from Jim, for several reasons.

When we were first married, Jim always encouraged me to pursue my career, to feel confident about myself and do my best. Ten years ago he encouraged me to go to Japan for a year to further not only my career, but my knowledge of the world. Since Jim's diagnosis, I think what's really given me strength is watching him be so courageous; if he wasn't that way I wouldn't have that strength. Also, his sense of humor. Throughout all of this Jim has humor, and it makes me realize that he's not afraid. It has changed the way I look at things.

Jim has always said, "I would like to die with dignity, I don't want to be hooked up to machines and I don't want to be in a rest home." But I never really had to face it until this happened. Jim and I have always been very supportive of each other. Throughout our marriage we've had some disagreements and differences, but we always support the way each other feels.

I am a religious person, and God has been my strength. Jim supports my religious beliefs and is very open to listening, and I'm the same way with him. He was supportive of the Death with Dignity Act in Oregon, and I was there for his wishes. It's not something I would do, but he is his own person. I remind him every day that today is another day, let's make the most of it, go somewhere, or take a walk with our dog.

JIM: When Kathy and I got married I had two boys and Kathy had two girls. They grew up together from the time they were three, four, five, and six. Now they are all in their twenties. My two sons are going out this spring to begin skydiving, and one son rides bicycles professionally. And the biggest joy in my heart is that today our kids are friends, they like each other, they do things together.

Now, all I do is look for things that make me happy. I make great martinis. We have a seven-month-old puppy, a golden retriever; I take her for a walk at night. It's enjoyable to see this puppy out there walking and the way she playfully gets on top of me and all over me. I like that.

KATHY: I try to help Jim enjoy each day. I think that because he has some enjoyment in life, and he can have some dignity in death, he wants to be here to enjoy it. His younger sister Dawn lived longer than the three or four months people usually live when they are diagnosed with pancreatic cancer. But she had a lot of suffering at the end.

JIM: Dawn also said she was looking forward to seeing Mother in heaven; I said, "I hope you do. But I don't buy that." I'm not a religious person.

I grew up in Salt Lake, and in the Mormon Church. I was in the Boy Scouts, played basketball, and went to church dances, but by age fourteen I could not accept the stories of the Christian religion. It's not that I said they're not true, I wanted proof. I will change my mind, my beliefs, as long as I know there's proof. My inner strength comes from knowing that I've done the right thing. I've tried to make a contribution to people my whole life. I've always tried to do things for other people, and the strength comes from my faith in people. I've got tremendous friends who are very compassionate, and I feel like I have a responsibility, especially to my family, but to my friends too, to stand tall and to be strong.

As for my students, even though I've been in the spotlight because of my role as school administrator, I never focused attention on me. I've always focused on the kids, and that's really important for me. I want my students to know that I believe in personal choice, and I believe very much in my right to choose to hasten my death. But I don't want the students to know I did it, because it's a very private personal matter, and I don't want them to think I committed suicide. I don't want the newspapers to say suicide.

Who knows, maybe I won't have to. I'm not sure how I would die naturally. Maybe with pneumonia, or choking to death. If I get to the point where I can't swallow, can no longer talk, can no longer breathe without a ventilator, and have a tracheotomy, a feeding tube—if I do go that far, I can still take the medication and put it in my feeding tube. It depends on the quality of life as every day goes by.

KATHY: Jim's disease has progressed, I think, fairly rapidly. There have been a few plateaus, but the plateaus were very short-lived. I would say there may be a month where things would be kind of okay. But then all of a sudden in the next couple of weeks he might lose strength in the other arm, or strength in the other leg, or his breathing would get worse. From the very beginning, his breathing has progressively been a problem. A year and a half ago he was on TV and he was walking around and now he can hardly take two steps without my help.

JIM: Right now I feel fine, but I lose a little bit of dignity every time I take a fall. I feel so bad about that because I used to jump out of airplanes at 12,000 feet. Now, I fall two feet to the ground and I think, *What the hell is wrong with me?* It hurts my pride to fall, but Kathy builds me up again.

KATHY: During the holidays, we had some people Jim worked with come over, and they asked if they could bring some kids who all knew Jim as their principal at one time or another. We said sure,

PHOTO: JOHN GRESS

I am so proud of Jim...
he stood up for
what he
believed in.
KATHY ROMNEY

bring them along. So a caravan of five cars pulls into our driveway
and about twenty people came in, and half of them were his students,
almost all boys, and they gave Mr. Romney hugs.

I think the way this has affected the kids is to think highly of Jim
for standing up for what he believes in. Maybe they don't believe it
themselves, but they really have admired him for that.

JIM: Great kids. They are so important to me. They email, write,
send pictures. Last year they asked me to speak at their graduation. I
said yes. I hadn't seen them since I hadn't been their principal for a
year, but of course I went to all their volleyball, basketball, and foot-
ball games. So at the graduation the new principal introduced me as
a speaker. Before I even said a word, there was a standing ovation
from all the kids, everybody, the whole gymnasium. I had to catch my
breath and dry my eyes before I could speak. Of course I told them
the reason that Rainier High School was the highlight of my life was
because of them. Then I thanked their parents, and everybody stood
up again for another ovation.

KATHY: This took place right after a whole year of Jim being very
public—being in magazines, newspapers, and on TV. There was
tremendous support for Jim. At that time Jim was not in a wheelchair

but he had a very hard time walking. He couldn't walk up to the stage area. Kids were sitting on the floor, facing the podium, so Jim walked up to the front, and just sat on the stairs. It was kind of neat because he wasn't up there behind a podium giving a speech. He was sitting there just talking with them, and one of the parents said that was the most meaningful graduation speech they had ever heard. His being there was so inspirational to the kids.

JIM: People who'd read about me in *People* magazine or the *Seattle Times* or other places have called me. Most were sales people. They wanted to wrap my body in magnets, or sell me certain remedies. One I met in a hospital emergency room said, "I've read about you. Drink lots of water, and use natural salt, and that will cure you of ALS."

One fellow who heard about my situation called to say that when he was a teenager his father had died of ALS, and he had terrible guilt feelings because his father asked him to take his life and he wouldn't do it. His dad was suffering so much, and none of the other family members would have anything to do with the dad. He was thinking about helping his dad end his life, but he didn't do it. He thanked me when I told him, "It's not your responsibility to take your father's life," and I thought he did the right thing. I would never ask my children to do that. If I could use their assistance, that's one thing, but I couldn't have them do it.

A woman I talked to said her father had a stroke, and one day he stepped in front of a train. She felt so bad about that. That's why I said a violent death is not helpful to the family.

When I am asked where my strength comes from, I tell them it comes from knowing that I've done the right thing. I've tried to make a contribution to people my whole life. When I was eighteen, I was coaching a Little League team. I've always tried to do things for other people, and the strength comes from my faith in people. I've got tremendous friends who are very compassionate, and I always feel like I have a responsibility, especially to my family, but to my friends too, to stand tall and to be strong.

When I was diagnosed with the disease, at first it was pretty upsetting, and I had some very sad moments. I am not in denial anymore, but now I know there is nothing I can do about it. Therefore, I have to look toward Kathy, our four children, our three grandkids, everybody else related, and to our friends, for the joy in life. That is all I do is look for things that make me happy. I have had a great life, I have always been very active, and I have done everything I could. I just love life.

Postscript
A TRIBUTE TO MY BELOVED HUSBAND, JIM

Four months after we had this interview, Jim died in a hospital with me at his side. My only regret is that he did not die at our home surrounded by our grown children and me. This is what he had always envisioned—how the end of his life would be a peaceful death with his loved ones around him.

Shortly after his death, I received an email from his friend and fellow school administrator. In it, he said (referring to his eulogy at Jim's service): "It was a privilege for me to be able to honor my friend and colleague who I admired and respected very much. Jim always stood up for what he believed was right for education and for kids, and he willingly accepted the risks that accompanied taking difficult and unpopular stands for his values. That's courage."

Jim had one more mission before his life was over…a mission that may have not been a popular stand with everyone. When he was diagnosed with ALS he wanted to make sure that Oregon's Death with Dignity law would still stand. He bravely faced TV cameras, reporters, and magazine editors to tell his story in hopes that people would understand his struggle with a terminal illness and that one should have a choice for end-of-life issues.

He fought that battle courageously until the end. Now Jim's struggle with ALS is over, and I am so proud of him for the fact that he stood up for what he believed in. Hopefully Jim made an impact on the future of many people in Oregon.

—KATHY

It's the freedom of choice that I feel so strongly about, freedom of being able to know your own destiny when you are dying and be able to choose when and where it's going to happen.

ROGER WATANABE

ROGER WATANABE

Two

Roger Watanabe

oger Dean Watanabe was born in 1947 in Ontario, Oregon, and grew up in this small agricultural town in Eastern Oregon dubbed "The Gateway to Oregon." He called Ontario the "Near East" because a large Japanese population had settled there after their release from Ontario's internment camp at the end of World War II. As a Japanese-American, Roger considered himself a "giant" among other Japanese because he was 5' 10" and weighed 180 pounds.

After two years of college Roger entered the Army. In 1969 and 1970 he worked as a counselor for an Army drug rehabilitation program called Head Way House at Fort Carson, Colorado. The program was the first of its kind, garnering national attention because it provided 24/7 drug counseling and treatment. Roger was part of a unit of counselors working with soldiers recently back from Vietnam, many with drug and combat-related problems. A longtime friend and colleague at the rehab center, Jeffrey Delia, recalls Roger as "a natural counselor. He had compassion and empathy for others' pain and their process. He was a good listener and never judged."

Counseling became Roger's life work during a career that included professional counseling at the Veterans Administration in Portland.

Roger's empathy and compassion stayed with him throughout his life, and when he faced his own suffering he displayed considerable compassion for himself, his family, and friends. He became the ultimate counselor and teacher for those who were close by while he was dying.

In August 1999, Roger received a diagnosis of Stage 3 colon cancer. A few months earlier, the mother of Roger's daughter had died from cancer. Roger had about two months to absorb her death before facing his own life-threatening cancer.

Roger had three surgeries and two rounds of chemotherapy in the hope of beating the disease. But by January 2002 the prognosis was terminal. Roger did not want to miss his own wake, so on a cold January day a few months before he died he hosted a gathering for thirty of his closest friends.

Crowded into a small apartment, they spent the evening celebrating Roger's life and saying good-bye. During the gathering his friends told stories from their pasts—coming of age in the 1960s, travels in Spain, working as drug counselors, testing their courage with fire walks, and more. Roger and his friends laughed, cried, drank, played guitars, and sang well into the night. But most importantly, they talked openly about Roger's impending death. One longtime friend said, "Here I am, going to my best man's wake. I've known Roger too long to believe that he wouldn't be at his own wake!" Another said, "Roger you are an embodiment of acceptance." And many times throughout the evening friends shared their appreciation and gratitude with Roger. "Roger, thanks for the good things you have given to all of your friends."

The following is an excerpt from the video made by his army friend Jeffrey Delia during Roger's final gathering with family and friends. Less than two months later, on March 11, 2002, Roger died peacefully and intentionally, surrounded by his loved ones, including some of his best Army buddies.

ROGER'S FINAL GATHERING

I can't tell you what it means to me to see all your faces here today. Some of you have known each other for years and some of you have never met at all—but I can say to all of you here today you are the people I have been closest to and loved for most of my life.

Many of you I've been friends with since I was a little child, some of you I have been good friends with for forty-five years. There are other friends here who I've known only a few days, but I've gotten close to you and collaborated with you. So, knowing someone for a length of time doesn't mean you are a better friend. A few days or a few decades are not necessarily relevant. To have all of you in the same room at the same time and of the same mind—and to sit down and talk with the people I love is incredible.

My good friend Bill—my wise and gray-haired friend—really encouraged me to do this. I don't know if I would have done it without his encouragement. We talked about what a special time this gathering would be. Now, I can see how true that really is.

When I was diagnosed with cancer I told some of my good friends that I didn't want to get to the point where I was totally dependent on people. I really didn't want to go on very long. I felt confident because I knew about Oregon's aid in dying law. Lo and behold, as my cancer progressed, when it was looking that it was pretty darn serious, and I wasn't going to beat this thing, U.S. Attorney General Ashcroft came along and said that he was going to stop this law and keep people in Oregon from using it. The Oregon aid in dying law is a national controversy because Ashcroft recently has tried to block this legislation—tried to block people in Oregon from doing this. Maybe this is totally coincidental, but maybe there are no coincidences with Ashcroft trying to stop the law in Oregon and my being sick right now.

It is the freedom of choice that I feel so strongly about, freedom of being able to know your own destiny when you are dying and be able to choose when and where it's going to happen. If I can do anything at all to ease people's minds about this legislation, to come out and talk about this, then I'll feel successful. The reason I can consider using aid in dying is because I've had a good life, I've had lots of good friends, I've seen parts of the world that a lot of people don't see. My life has been full. I don't feel bad about my passing into this next phase.

My strongest hope is that you won't be afraid of death. If I can help people accept their aging process, and the process of their own dying, as natural, then I will be happy. The hospice people I work with tell me that this kind of work is similar to working with newborns. The cycle goes on.

It is surrealistic to be talking about possibly using the law. One of the reasons I wanted to have this gathering was to let people know that until the event actually occurs, I don't know if I'll do it. I can't know for sure until the time when I take the drug and say good-bye to this world and hello to the next world. I feel strongly about having the choice to use the law.

There are only a few pharmacies in the metro area that will fill the prescription. I took my prescription to one of these pharmacies. When I went in and introduced myself to the pharmacist he looked right at me, shook my hand, and told me he was glad to meet me and said my prescription was ready. He gave me a bottle of a liquid barbiturate. He was pretty serious— it's not like going in for some antibiotics. I wanted to joke around with this pharmacist and pull his leg a bit. I was going to say, "Listen, are there any bad side effects to this? Is it okay to drive with this?" But he was such a nice guy I couldn't pull it off.

Fortunately, now that I have the actual medication I don't have any worries. Ashcroft or anyone else cannot block me. If I do decide to take the medication to end my life, no one can be prosecuted—my doctors, the pharmacists, anyone who helps me cannot be prosecuted. That is a great relief to me.

Another reason I wanted to have the gathering is to let people know how strongly I feel about my own demise and other people's deaths. This subject interested me long before I was diagnosed with cancer. I always wanted to ask someone who was dying, "Are you afraid? What does it feel like to face death, to look the grim reaper right in the face?" But out of politeness, I have never asked. It's tough to ask those questions, even if the person is a close friend.

Every person who has ever been on this earth has gone through dying. Everyone who is here today will face death, and many of our parents are sick or gone. So I always thought that when I faced my own death I was going to let other people know what I thought about it. It's okay to talk about it. I encourage people to talk about it. It helps the person die and hopefully helps those around who are sad. So another reason for this gathering is to make it easier on your own death, or the death of anyone you love, to simply say it is okay to talk about this or to tell them that you love them.

We have all been in the situation of not knowing what to say to someone who was dying. Now I'm the sick one who is dying, and I can say anything I want. And I can encourage other people to ask me questions. Don't hesitate to interrupt me, ask a question, or to make a comment. There may not be a heck of a lot of tomorrows for me. I am not very afraid to die.

Be sad that I'm dying but it's nothing that ain't going to happen to every single person. I'm not afraid of dying and I'm not in great pain—but I am afraid of suffering. The closer I get to death the pain medication will get stronger. I have three hospice nurses working with me, all are men and all are totally supportive of what I want to do.

When you have a life-threatening disease it brings out your issues. Your spirituality comes to the surface. The material things don't matter to me now. Father Ram Dass is a teacher who talks about living in the Now, living in the present. I think I'm learning to do that more than anything else. When you have a life-threatening disease and you know that life is going to be finite, it brings you to the Now. If you have issues—good or bad—tell people that you love them, It helps life get more real.

That is why I wanted to gather all of you together today. I want to tell you how much I love all of you and how much I appreciate all you've done for me over the past few months. I don't want to scare you away because I am dying. I want you to know I am not afraid. I am saying, "Come on, I'm ready for death." I have never been real religious but I have always thought of myself as a spiritual person. I have always believed there was something good on the other side.

I want to say to the people of Oregon, "Thank you. Thank you for your vote. You don't know how wonderful it is to have that law here tonight when I'm going to use it."

PENNY SCHLEUTER

PENNY SCHLEUTER

Three

Penny Schleuter

Penelope "Penny" Schleuter described herself as "ornery enough" to fight the spread of her cancer—and she was ornery enough to fight for the right of Oregonians to choose a death with dignity.

As late as the month before she died, Penny was speaking out in defense of Oregon's assisted dying law. Even when sitting in a chair or standing became too painful, she continued to fight. "When I'm no longer alive but not dead yet," she explained, "I want the option to die with dignity." Penny drew a distinction between life and "mere existence" and she had no desire to spend time in the latter state.

Penny was born in 1941 in Riverside, California. She graduated in 1963 from Miami University in Oxford, Ohio, and earned a master's degree in economics at Washington State University in 1968. For twenty-three years she taught economics at Lane Community College in Eugene. She served on the board of Pacific Northwest Regional Economic Conference and on the Oregon Council on Economic Education as well as on an educational committee for the Federal Reserve Board of San Francisco.

Penny's five-year struggle against ovarian cancer began in 1993. Doctors initially diagnosed her abdominal pain as an intestinal condition and this error cost precious months of delayed treatment.

Penny pursued every available cancer treatment, including participation in clinical trials for Taxol, which kept the disease in check more than three years. But even as she struggled to live she drew comfort from knowing that if she lost her battle with cancer, she would be able to choose a peaceful, dignified death for herself under Oregon's Death with Dignity Act.

For Penny, aid in dying was like auto insurance: "When you buy insurance for your car you certainly don't plan to get in an accident just to use that policy." She believed that just having the choice could help people have the courage to stay alive and deal with whatever suffering their disease brought them. It frustrated her when opponents of the Act argued that terminally ill people wanted to die. "They don't understand that most terminally ill people don't give up. We don't want to die. We just don't want to linger in unbearable pain, just existing."

Having this option was so important to her that even while she underwent chemotherapy she traveled to Oregon's capital, Salem, to explain to lawmakers why she supported physician aid in dying and why she opposed the legislators who wanted to repeal the law. At one hearing she told them, "The idea that my choice to use the Death with Dignity Act might be taken away from me makes me angry and anxious."

Throughout the state Penny became a recognized advocate for Oregon's aid in dying law. She appeared in campaign advertisements and newspaper stories, including the front page of the *New York Times*. She gave countless interviews to local and national reporters after the law was passed and during attempts to repeal it. She defended not only the right of the individual to have a full range of medical options at the end of life, but also the will of the Oregon citizens who had voted for and approved the law. Her courageous stand helped persuade Oregonians to reject the call for repeal and vote once again in support of the law. And all the while she contended with ongoing cancer treatment and increasing pain, weakness, and debilitation of her body from the cancer.

Those who knew Penny admired her strength, wisdom, and courage. Even at the end of her life she continued to speak out for end-of-life choice. Her best friend described Penny as "a strong, compassionate, dedicated person who cared for life and for other people. She was a great instructor, and she never quit teaching, even after she retired. I think she went to the grave instructing and that's just the way she'd want it."

On Penny's last night, she talked with me at length about many things, including her passionate belief in Oregon's aid in dying law, her advocacy on behalf of the law, and her declining health. We had become good friends as well as colleagues in our public efforts in Oregon. So to spend this final evening with Penny was a special sadness as well as a special honor. On September 22, 1998, Penny died at the age of fifty-seven at her home in Pleasant Hill, Oregon, using the law she fought for so passionately.

PENNY SCHLEUTER

I have finally gotten to the point that I don't feel I'm living but just existing. At times I have pain, but the control is there to take over and keep it from getting bad. But what is really bad, and what can't be controlled, are the side effects. I'm having serious problems with energy. A little bit of exertion and I'm panting. People who know me can tell by my voice and the way I'm talking that I'm short on oxygen. I'm also very anemic, so that any sort of activity really wears me out. My biggest problem is incontinence. I have absolutely, positively no control over my bladder or my bowels. They just continuously run. I have to wear adult diapers. I am never clean. I can take a shower and be cleaned up, and two minutes later I'm dirty again.

I'm getting to the point where I need help standing up, getting out of a chair. I don't have the strength in my legs to push myself to get up. My balance has gotten pretty bad in the last week and I've taken a couple of bad falls. This seems to happen without warning. I'm at the point where I almost need someone with me twenty-four hours a day to keep me from falling, to help clean up the messes, and to basically help me move because I cannot move myself to where I want to go. That's not living, that's just existing. I don't want to live this way. I don't want to have to have twenty-four-hour care. I've lived alone most of my life. I like doing things for myself, and the idea of having somebody take care of me like I am a little two-month-old baby is just absolutely repulsive. It's more painful than any of the pain from the cancer.

There were many people who helped get the assisted dying law passed in Oregon. My contribution was a small part of a large job that required many people. There's still so much work to be done. Tonight

I want to say to the people of Oregon, "Thank you. Thank you for your vote. Thank you for your support. You don't know how wonderful it is to have that law here tonight when I'm going to use it." I feel so very sorry for the people over the last four years who could have used the law but didn't because of the court stay that was in effect.

In 1997, a few months before the election, I spoke at the Eugene City Club's Fall program. They were having a panel discussion on the Death with Dignity Act and had formed a committee to look at whether the ballot measure should be voted for or against. The repeal measure was badly worded; if you voted yes, it meant you were against assisted suicide, and if you voted no, that meant you were for it. The committee wanted to hear both sides. Geoff Sugarman, an advocate for the law, and I represented the position in favor of assisted dying.

At the time I was testifying I was beginning to feel the effects of the cancer more. Up until then I had been managing it. I was still able to drive a car by using a special cushion, and when I sat in chairs I used a neck cushion. I would select particular chairs when I'd go into a room because I knew some of them were very painful to sit in. I had to be quite careful, though, and couldn't do long drives or attend long meetings because it became too painful. But I could attend local meetings such as the City Club.

We spoke first for about an hour and gave the committee members brochures to read. They asked very good questions, ones that focused on the philosophy of physician-aided dying. They stayed away from the strictly religious aspects of the issue, which can get quite rabid. They did, of course, look at it from the moral perspective, but they also asked about concerns that had been raised in the campaign, such as how long people could linger and the pills they would take.

In the end, the City Club was very supportive of the law, voting very heavily for our side. By that time I was pretty seasoned as a supporter since I had already gone through the legislative session. [In March 1997, Penny testified before the Oregon Legislature's Senate subcommittee that was considering repeal of the law.] If the politicians would concentrate on better pain management for the terminally ill and let people decide for themselves, we'd all be better off.

That legislative session was very tough. During the May 1997 hearings the legislators wouldn't look me in the eye, particularly when I first testified. When I first sat down, no one knew me because I'd never been active in the legislature. I was truly an unknown face. My hair was thinning quite a bit because I was on chemotherapy. I was wearing a hat and was a little bent over and when I first stood up to testify, I think some thought I was a little old grandmother. When I said I was an ovarian cancer patient, everyone perked up and looked at me. And then, when I said that I was supportive of Oregon's Death with Dignity law, why, all of a sudden a whole bunch of eyes looked down. They never looked me in the eye again.

That was a hard time. One representative promised me three things: no repeal, no referral, and no major revisions that would change the real meaning of the law. And then he went back on his word. Well, let's just say he's not in my good thoughts tonight.

But it was another state representative who bothered me the most. During one of the committee meetings I met him out in the hall and wanted to talk to him. I knew he was a policeman and I knew that policemen hate to go out on suicide calls because they can be so messy. I tried to use that as a way of talking to him. He just brushed it off, saying that people shouldn't do it, shouldn't take their own life. I said, "But you know that they're going to do it anyway, no matter what the law is."

His response was, "Well, that's their business." Then I said how hard it was on the family—that often the family wants to be there at the bedside, but they can't for fear they'll be arrested or charged with assisting suicide. I also said that if the suicide is done with something such as a gun it's a very messy affair. And his response, made in a very flippant way, was, "That's their choice." So then I said, "What about the doctors who could prescribe medicine but risked losing their license, just by being compassionate and caring." Again he was flippant, saying, "Well, that's their choice." Then he just walked away. For someone who claimed to be a compassionate person—and he kept saying about how compassionate he was—he was showing absolutely no compassion.

I was really motivated to become involved when the state legislature decided to hold hearings to repeal the law while it was still under court injunction. I thought it terrible that the law had been under court injunction for three years in the first place. It didn't have to be delayed that long. I felt the slowness of the courts was a deliberate way of keeping the law from going into effect. Then the state legislature decided to try and repeal it even before the court ruling. For me, that was the straw that broke the camel's back. I was mad. I asked the Death with Dignity people what I could do. They said, "Testify."

I had never testified before. I'd never even been very active in politics. I watched an afternoon's worth of testimony and saw how things worked in the legislature. I was very upset with some of the blatant lies that were being told. When I went home that evening I jotted down some notes. The next day I went back and testified before the legislature. I got involved because the legislature finally went too far and got me so angry that I had to do something.

I was surprised at the number of reporters who, after interviewing me, said, "I have some problems with the law, and I could never personally use it, but basically I support your position." I am still surprised at the number of people who would come up and say, "I voted against it the first time, but I voted for it the second time." Many of them considered it arrogance on the part of the legislature to go against the vote of the people without even offering revisions. The legislature could have put up an amended version for a vote and been less arrogant.

There have been two votes by the citizens of Oregon. The first vote was fairly close because of all the scare tactics. The second vote was such a strong affirmation of what the Oregon voters want and I really don't see how a legislator can, with a straight face, say he or she prefers to repeal the law. Most of the national surveys show that people support the law. It is the politicians who, for some reason, seem more willing to support the very vocal religious groups who think they can save the souls of the wayward. But they should pay attention to their own souls.

The more time that passes, the more support there seems to be for the law. People have had a chance to think about it, and to see that some of the wild tales the opponents told aren't coming true. Doctors are not flocking to Oregon to build dormitories so people can establish six-month residencies before committing suicide. They assume the worst of people who support Death with Dignity. Those who are considering using the Death with Dignity Act don't want to die alone in the middle of nowhere—they want to end their lives in their homes with their family and friends around them.

I want the security of knowing the option is there. After Attorney General Janet Reno said the Drug Enforcement Agency should not get involved, that it was a states' rights issue, I felt great comfort. Now I am filled with contentment and peace I simply didn't have when the law was tied up in the courts.

From a spiritual perspective I feel we have brains, we have an intellect. We can reason. If we don't use our brains then we're not really using our full human capabilities. So I think this decision is one for each person to reason, to think about, and to draw his or her own conclusions.

FROM LEFT: JULIE, ELLEN, ANNE, KATHLEEN, RICHARD, AND PEGGY

The Death with Dignity Act
is all about choice.
My advice to a family in
this situation is to
respect the wishes of the
terminally ill.
It's their issue.

JULIE MCMURCHIE
DAUGHTER

Four

Margaret "Peggy" Haas Sutherland

Margaret Haas Sutherland—Peggy—was an independent thinker. A graduate of Mount Holyoke College in philosophy and psychology, she was considered smart and strong-willed. She also placed a high value on self-sufficiency and encouraged this in her five children. Those who knew Peggy say she was tolerant, accepting, encouraging, and intellectually curious. She questioned authority, and she believed people can do anything they set their minds to. Peggy instilled a love of music in her family and she loved to dance. She played the piano and especially enjoyed classical music and opera. But her tastes encompassed jazz, gospel hymns, Harry Belafonte, and the Irish Rovers.

Peggy was born in White Plains, New York in 1932, and moved with her family to Pennsylvania when she was six years old. After college she married Donald Sutherland, a physician, and they had four girls and a boy. The family moved to Oregon in 1961 and Peggy immersed herself in community activity in addition to caring for her growing family. Peggy was active on the boards of the Portland Chamber Orchestra, Chamber Music Northwest, and the Colonial Dames of America; a founding member of the Oregon Psychoanalytic Foundation and a volunteer at Hopewell House, a Portland hospice.

In January 2000, at age sixty-seven, Peggy found out she had lung cancer. Nearly one year later, after two surgeries and intensive cancer treatment, Peggy knew she was approaching death. One of her lungs was removed and the cancer had eaten away a rib. Peggy was coughing up blood, and the pain grew more intense despite strong medication. She decided the time had come to determine when she would die. For this, she turned to Compassion in Dying.

Throughout Peggy's process of choosing aid in dying, her family was involved, learning everything they could and talking with their mother. Peggy's children supported her wish to control her own death, but one of her children who is a physician realized she would not be willing to prescribe medications for assisted dying to her own patients. However, she did acknowledge and respect her mother's personal decision to end her life.

Peggy Sutherland ingested the prescribed medication on January 25, 2001. She was surrounded by family and friends, at peace in her own home, looking out the window at the Willamette River as it meandered through Portland. The following stories are by four of Peggy's children and one grandchild.

JULIE MCMURCHIE
Daughter, homemaker, and mother of three children

My mother was so clear. It wasn't a process of us deciding, it was her decision. It wasn't our choice to make. She was a competent, intelligent woman. It was not for me to tell her what to do. Besides, I supported her. I never once felt that I shouldn't help her to do this;

I don't think any of my siblings did either. I remember a few conversations with my siblings who are doctors, Dick and Kathy, about the Hippocratic Oath. I remember them saying, "This is something I always assumed I would not do." But it was a complication, never a conflict. Nobody argued that we should not do this. It's not that we are a no-conflict family, but on this, it was Mom's decision and we all respected that. For God's sake, the woman had just been through hell for a year. How could we tell her she had no burdens? It was obvious to me.

I get so upset when I hear people say, "All you need is a doctor who will take care of the pain." My mother's final words when she took the drug were, "I don't think anyone has understood the pain I have been in." She'd had two lung surgeries prior to the terminal diagnosis. Those are really painful. They cut from your back through your nerves. She had just recovered from one, then had to have another, and just recovered from that and found she was terminally ill. It was really about pain. She had been bedridden for six weeks. She had a morphine pump in her spine, and we never got it to where she was stable enough to get to the beach again. It became clear during those three weeks in the hospital at Christmas of 2000 that she was going to die. That was when the emphasis shifted from doing everything we could to keep her alive to allowing her to die. She had made veiled references to assisted suicide for several months, saying things like, "I'm glad I live in Oregon."

Her decision to use the Death with Dignity Act was never a secret. I went to every doctor's appointment with her. I was there constantly the last few weeks. The internist, oncologist, radiation specialist, surgeons, and the pulmonologist all knew. We were lucky to be so medically sophisticated.

On January 25 she was in her own apartment, looking out the window at the Willamette River. She had already said goodbye to her bridge partners and old college classmates. Her children and their spouses were with her, and her best friend, her sister, and her nephew. She kissed us, and Dick read the Twenty-third Psalm—she insisted on the King James Version. Then she took the Seconal. In five minutes she was unconscious, and in fifteen minutes she was dead.

I was so involved that right after she died I was having flashbacks of all the terrible moments and I think it really helped me progress in my grieving to be able to talk about it. I feel lucky because I can talk about it now, two years later. It's still there, and often I think of things she would enjoy, I wish she could be here, I wish I could tell her. But I don't carry a big, dark, ugly thing.

The Death with Dignity Act is all about choice. My advice to a family in this situation is to respect the wishes of the terminally ill. It's their issue. I think it's okay to express your opinion to the person, but respectfully. Let your own beliefs be your own beliefs. My mother was very open that she was dying. I think that made it easier for all of us. We were all emotionally present in her dying. I would never presume to exert my control over an intellectually competent person. We all are entitled to our own decisions.

KATHLEEN SUTHERLAND
Daughter, pulmonary and critical care physician, and mother of two children

I work in the medical community, and I have been with patients when they died. I thought we could manage the end of my mother's life with good pain control, hospice care, and nursing care that she had the funds for. That was the place I was coming from. I was not real keen on my mother using physician assisted dying at the beginning, but I could definitely understand why she wanted to. When it came down to it, I could see that my mom's quality of life was not going to be good for those last weeks of her life, so I was okay with her decision.

As a doctor, I would never write a prescription for this medication. It is not a service I want to provide for patients. Do I believe that this service should be available? Yes. Am I willing to refer my patients to another physician and a psychiatrist? Absolutely. But it is not something I would do.

I thought the epidural catheter would work better for her pain than it did and she would be able to go to the beach for a few weeks before she died. My mom had periods when she was better; we went to the Oregon Coast the week before Thanksgiving. Then she got precipitously worse very quickly from Thanksgiving to Christmas.

I think she was very much at peace with dying. Mom wanted to be in control of the moment she died, and she wanted to be with all her children and the people who were important to her. She had lost all hope. She did not feel there was anything worth living for, because she had to be on so much pain medication she could barely carry on a conversation. She didn't see any point to staying alive that way for another six weeks.

My mother was a very strong-willed person and she wanted to be in control during the time of her death; that's why this law was important to her. To me that was more important than the daily pain issue. I was with her and I think her pain was pretty well controlled by the end. That was my perception. I can't speak as knowledgeably about it; pain is a complicated thing.

The Death with Dignity Act is a good law, I could see that. My mother was psychologically astute and medically sophisticated. I don't think the law would have been abused or misinterpreted in our family setting. We were fortunate that our mother was already seeing a psychiatrist before she got her illness, so we were able to use his evaluation, along with the other referring physicians, to say that she was not clinically depressed. I thought the law worked very well for our family. We all had a very close relationship with my mom and we didn't have any conflict or debate about whether Mom should do this or not; she was in charge.

My sister Ann is a pretty highly functioning mentally retarded person, meaning that her IQ is in the high 70s to 80s range, and so she could process all this. She understood that Mom had cancer, she knew that Mom was going to die. She had long talks with Mom about it. I don't recall having a conversation with Ann where she expressed any concern about this choice. Ann wanted facts: what's going to happen, how soon will she die, when will we know she's dead. She would cry.

I really didn't want my mother to die. I was very close to her and I loved her very much. I valued my time with her. I went through all the stages of anger and grief, and I was able to come around to getting comfortable with it when I realized this was going to happen whether I liked it or not—my mother was going to die.

It was really that process of being there a lot, spending so much time with my mother at the end of her life, that let me understand why she wanted to do this. If I had not done that I probably would have always been uncomfortable with it.

If I were to counsel a family in this situation I would say it would be very important for each child to spend enough time with the person who wanted to use the law, talking to them and learning as much about the law and the process as possible. That was the most valuable thing for me.

Everyone should be in charge of their own life, and they should get to die in a way that is comfortable for them. Mom was a unique person. She died honorably in the way she wanted to die. It was the right thing for her.

ELLEN BALTUS
Daughter, social worker, and mother of two children

We live in a society that tells us to not talk about dying: just caretake and say all is well, and don't ask direct questions. But my mother was incredibly direct. She always told us, "When things get uncomfortable or difficult you talk about it." In our family we talked. To not talk about her dying would have been weird.

After Mom got a terminal diagnosis, months ahead of her death I felt we could talk about her dying. We would ask questions like, "So what are you going to do with the time before you die? How are you going to live to your fullest? How are we going to make you the most comfortable?"

We told her, "When you get to the point that you feel you no longer have control, we're going to make sure we have a prescription for you so you don't have to live in misery."

I wish we had done it sooner, to be honest. I wish we had gotten the prescription a month earlier, filled it, and had it there. Mom should have taken it days before. I think it would have prevented the suffering she had. People can say it was only a couple of days she suffered badly, but it was awful. She suffered. Mom talked about the frustration she felt that no one would ever understand the degree of pain she had been in. I was there, and I slept on the floor next to her bed the night she died. She was waking up in these weird morphine states, half awake and half asleep, crying out, having bowel movements. Nobody should have to live like that, especially a woman with such incredible class. It takes away all sense of dignity. My mother was a classy and dignified woman.

I suspected from the start that my mother would probably choose assisted dying. She was a very decisive person who was never afraid to face and discuss difficult issues. Mom's attitude was, "This is how I feel about dying. This feels awful, I don't want to die that way, I want to get the prescription...." She also talked about other details, such as when to die, how she saw it happening, and what she wanted read at the time of her death. It was more than just the assisted dying, it was the process of death, too. When you feel like you have choice, then you feel like everything isn't out of control, or worried every second that you could die at any moment. This way, it feels like you can be comforted in the process.

I have always supported the Death with Dignity law and believe it is an individual's right to have that choice at the end of their life. My brother and sister, both doctors, had a discussion on how to help someone die when you're a physician. It goes against the oath you take, but we weren't battling this. There was no conflict among the siblings; it was our own personal "how do you get around it?" For me it would be a good choice if I knew I were going to die. I want to live, I want to be with the people I love as long as I can. But if I were in pain I would choose the assisted dying law. That's what my mother chose.

There was a lot of love for my mom, unconditional love. The weaknesses, the little things that bugged me about my mom became totally irrelevant towards the end of her life because I knew I only had a little more time with her, so I just loved her. My attitude became, "What do you need, Mom? What can I do for you today?"

My mother gave me many gifts throughout her life. They include the gift of acceptance of others and love for divergent thinking. She gave us opportunities to stretch. By the age of eight or nine all of us children were doing our own laundry, a lesson toward self-sufficiency. By the time we went to college we each knew that Mom expected us to take care of ourselves and face any personal challenges. She expected that we would be successful and today we are.

She encouraged our friends to speak openly about difficult and controversial subjects. I loved it when my friends would get into debates and heart-to-hearts with my mom, and so did she. She loved those who did not fit the mold. I felt accepted.

Mom also gave me the gift of music. When we traveled to the beach as a family, Mom would teach us songs and harmonies. Each of my sisters and brother would take a part. Even in the last years of Mom's life her appreciation for music did not dwindle. She went to concerts, performances of Chamber Music Northwest, the opera, jazz, and gospel music. She played music, she sang, and she encouraged her family to include music in their lives. I felt very close to Mom in those last few months and I am very grateful to God that I had the time to share with her all that I needed to before she died. When the day came and everyone who adored her was with her, I was full of love and acceptance for what she was doing. I could see in her face the relief she felt in being able to finally end the suffering. It was a beautiful thing, people were very open.

I remember feeling surprised at how clear-minded Mom seemed the morning of her death, lucid and happy. Different passages were read from the Bible, Shakespeare, and a poet she liked. I watched her take it in, seeming so relaxed and ready. I remember feeling like we needed to take care of my sister Ann, who is retarded, to make sure she was okay. Mom reassured Ann.

After Mom drank the medicine she fell asleep almost immediately. We watched her as we cried and comforted Ann. The doctor checked her pulse, and again later, and stated the time of death. People began to leave, going downstairs. I did not want to leave the room until they took her body. I did not want Mom to ever have to be alone, even though I knew intellectually she was gone. I felt she needed someone to stay with her body until it was out of her home. Mom deserved to be protected until the last possible moment. When they put her body in the van and drove away, I felt like my job of caring for her physically was finally over.

It is hard to put into words how powerful the experience is, watching someone you need and adore die, and yet be glad. My love was without boundaries and unconditional. I wanted my mom to be given comfort and to be free from pain even if it meant she was no longer in my life.

I would advise people in this situation to get the prescription early. People don't want to use it until they absolutely have to, they want to live. And if they know they have that choice, than they want to live every moment that they can.

RICHARD SUTHERLAND
Son, physician, and father of two children

I was completely in favor of my mother's decision. There was never a question in my mind; I am and was always comfortable with it. I have always believed in the value of assisted dying, but in reality my personal beliefs about it have little if anything to do with the decisions of an intelligent, competent person who is in pain and dying. Any questions I might have if I were put in that situation are irrelevant. The only potential difficulty with her decision would have been if a new drug or procedure were discovered that would have definitely cured her cancer, and she chose to take the barbiturate instead.

A concern my sisters and I had was whether one of us should object to her decision, just to see if she was unsure of her decision and not telling us. We wondered if maybe she was seeing if anyone would give her support if she wanted to change her mind. None of us, that I know of, objected to her decision, but it was a way to check if she had doubts. But when she was confronted on the days when she could talk because she withheld her morphine, she was clearly confident of her decision.

What I would tell a family placed in our situation is, "Life isn't fair." At some point a terrible thing occurs, which rips someone from you. Realize that, and move on to the next phase of helping that person cope with the tragedy. This is about the person, not you. As mad or angry or afraid as you are, the real focus is on the dying individual.

Assisted suicide may or may not be the best way. There may be other ways to bring emotional comfort and relief to the person. When everything is over and done and your loved one has passed on, the family will cope best by knowing they did everything they could to comfort, love, and help the individual in need.

Assisted suicide is an action; you are taking your own life and should be clear why and when that should, if ever, occur. Many people are incapable of that action. No one can create, teach, or produce this feeling in an individual. Many people who know they are dying from a malignancy and what that entails, still choose, rightly, not to act. It is their decision. But if your loved one does not want to be bedridden with severe pain and fogged mentally from narcotics, having their feces cleaned by family members daily with no hope of change until they die in that very room, then assisted suicide is potentially a very good option.

My mother was a very insightful and intelligent person when it came to the psychological and emotional make-up of people and what makes one tick. There is simply not another person in my life whom I can talk to like I could with her. The "mumbo jumbo" of psychoanalysis was a fluid language with her, and I miss those discussions. I have other thoughts, emotions, and reflections that come and go as I think of my mother's death. They are all good because I know she passed away in a manner that made her happy, surrounded by her family who loved her. She wasn't happy she had cancer, she wasn't happy to be denied life and playing with her grandchildren. But again, life isn't always fair. Make the best of your situation. She did.

LINDSAY BALTUS
Granddaughter, thirteen, wrote this story one year after her grandmother's death. She is Ellen's daughter.

QUESTIONING ANOTHER DEATH

My Grandma Peggy used to smoke. A lot. She'd do that thing where you smoke a cigarette and then when it's almost out you light a new one with the burning end of the butt. Chain-smoking.

She'd smoke all day when my mom and my mom's siblings were little, smoke all day inside the house and read novels and put together puzzles. Then she got lung cancer. It was before I was born, before my parents' wedding, and she stopped smoking. She had to have a big part of one lung removed, but she lived and the cancer was gone.

Then, years later when I was about eleven, we learned that the cancer had come back. She hadn't had a cigarette for fifteen years, but she went to have her lungs checked out and there was the telltale black spot. Big and ugly, dark like a grave. I remember we were at an Italian restaurant a little while after my mom found out, and in the middle of dinner my mom started to cry. "Grandma has cancer," she said. "My mother has lung cancer again, and I'm afraid."

Photo: Ellen Baltus

GRANDMA PEGGY AND LINDSAY

We were all afraid. Grandma was getting thinner and paler all the time. At first we hoped that the cancer could be destroyed. The doctors tried chemotherapy, and all of Grandma's amazing naturally dark hair started to fall out. They removed all of one lung, so she was left with half the air a person should be able to breathe and had to have one of those scary oxygen tanks. A year went by, and she was not getting better. Time after time we got a phone call from the hospital or from one of my aunts saying that Grandma Peggy had to be readmitted.

My thirteenth Christmas was spent at St. Vincent's Hospital. The hospital is a very scary place with its cold hallways and strange smells. It is even scarier when your grandmother, who you love very much, is lying in front of you, all white and bony like a skeleton with tubes plugged into her. Grandma was only half-conscious, her eyes fluttering open and closed. While we sat in uncomfortable teal leather-upholstered chairs, staring at the dully wallpapered walls, she gave us our Christmas gifts. My brother had a huge bag of gold dollar coins. He was ecstatic. She gave me money, too, but I also got a pretty little velvet box. Inside it was a dried rose and a tiny bird's nest. There was also a figurine of a sitting fairy. Grandma couldn't walk anymore, so I knew that she must have seen this fairy awhile ago while shopping and thought of me. In that funny smelling little hospital room, I finally realized that my grandmother, Grandma Peggy, who loved me and knew everything about the world, was going to die soon.

Grandma was in pain and everyone knew it. She told her children that she knew she was going to die and didn't want to suffer any longer. She was prescribed a fatal dose of barbiturates, which she took on January 25, 2001, exactly a month after Christmas. She said goodbye to her four daughters and one son, fell asleep, and died peacefully.

Her death was a controversial one. Assisted suicide is a big deal right now. My mother and aunts are still being interviewed about it, over a year after Grandma's death. They've been in numerous newspapers and this week they will be on ABC News. We are all constantly being reminded that she's gone. I guess it's good for us, but sometimes it hurts. It's been hard for them without Grandma, I can tell, and it's been hard for me too. Last Christmas there was something missing. There was no one with colorful, flowing skirts and sophisticated perfume. There was no one to talk to about opera, no one around who I could ask any question in the world to and receive an answer like an encyclopedia entry.

Grandma loved to see me act. Sometimes onstage or during rehearsals I wonder if she can watch my plays from where she is. I think she would have wanted the way she died to spark interest. I bet she likes that people are still talking about her, that she made them think and question what they believe. Grandma Peggy liked to stimulate people's minds, and she's still good at it.

Five

A Compassion Volunteer's Perspective

ichaele Wilk Houston has been a volunteer with Compassion in Dying of Oregon since 2000. She was strongly influenced to pursue this work after the death of her father in 1988, who, prior to his death, encouraged Michaele to start volunteer work as a support group facilitator for people facing a life-threatening illness. Soon afterward, she began facilitating a support group for men diagnosed with AIDS under the auspices of the not-for-profit Cascade AIDS Project (CAP). All eighteen members of that support group died. "I sat with many of them through their dying," explains Michaele, "acting as a kind of 'death coach' much the same way a midwife supports the birthing process."

Later, Michaele cared for a dear friend who was dying of AIDS. He lived with her for three years, and they married in the final year of his life. Subsequently, Michaele began working with Compassion. The following are some of her experiences from the volunteer work she refers to as a "calling."

MICHAELE HOUSTON

My journey is similar to the path that leads almost all volunteers to Compassion—we want to do this work because we have experienced death, good and bad, and we know the difference. We want to help people achieve an end to their life that is peaceful and dignified—a death they define for themselves.

Compassion is not an advocacy organization for physician assisted death, it is an advocacy organization for choice. If that choice is a hastened death, we do not flinch or turn away. Unqualified support is very important to the clients we serve, and for some, it is the ultimate answer to the question, "How can I help?"

Working with people at the end of their lives is an honor and a privilege. Being present with people grappling with end-of-life issues and, in many cases, being with them at their death, is, at once, simple and complex. It is frequently challenging, sometimes difficult, but always fulfilling.

All volunteers at Compassion are trained and supervised until they are experienced enough to mentor new volunteers. But the truth is this: when you decide you want to do this work, you bring everything you need with you. People offer many reasons for why they want to volunteer, but when they have the greatest clarity, they will tell you it is almost a calling.

People at the end of life are often at their most vulnerable and their most honest. They demand similar honesty from you. If you are prepared to open your heart, to meet people where they are, and to offer help in whatever form they ask, relationships of great warmth and emotional intimacy can develop quickly.

People choose to use Oregon's Death with Dignity law infrequently. Most who become Compassion clients and receive volunteer support team services do not get their lethal prescriptions. Many get their prescriptions and do not use them. Almost all Compassion clients tell us they feel more secure and at peace knowing they will not be abandoned should they choose a hastened death.

In my three years with Compassion, I have been a volunteer support person for more than forty people, including twenty whose hastened deaths I attended. Each taught me something important, leaving memories I will cherish all my life.

One such person was James, a world famous psychiatrist in his seventies, who had studied Eastern religions with many of the masters. He had pancreatic cancer and had chosen not to have surgery or chemotherapy. He asked to meet with me once a week. Each time, we engaged in intense dialogues about life, death, meaning and purpose, hopes and fears. When he got tired, he would end the discussion. After about six weeks, I realized he was ending each of our talks after a fifty-minute discussion. Even as he lived his dying, he was doing it in the context of the therapeutic "Fifty-Minute Hour."

James had his prescription but never chose to use it. He said it was liberating to know his death could be in his control. He used this freedom from fear to finish a list of things important to him, including a talk with each of his eight children about what he thought his life had meant and hearing from each of them how he had influenced their lives.

James planned his memorial service, named his tumor so he could get to know it better, and spent many hours expressing gratitude to his wife, his family, and the cosmos. I was privileged to watch him move from a place of fear to one of peace and acceptance. On the day he died, he told me he loved me and thanked me for asking him such good questions.

During his dying process, James and his wife, Joan, lived with Joan's sister Martha. Two years later, Joan called to say Martha was dying. Martha wanted to talk with me as I had done with James because he had found it so helpful. I was honored to visit with her several times a week until her death. She never intended to hasten her death but she was a Compassion client nonetheless.

I will always remember Frank, a sweet and gentle man in his late seventies. He had been fiercely independent all of his life and prided himself on being the person in his family who cared for his parents in their final illnesses. Frank had never married and had no surviving family, except one niece. His cancer was quickly advancing and he refused to die in a nursing home. He knew he couldn't care for himself much longer. He wanted to die in his own home and wanted Compassion's help to make sure the process went smoothly. Although his niece supported his decision to hasten his death, she could not bring herself to be present when Frank died. The day Frank decided to die, he knew he did not want to die alone. When Sue, another Compassion volunteer, and I arrived at his home, he was in the parking lot waiting for us. Frank was wearing what he later told us were his best pants and shirt because, "Today is a special occasion."

He sat in the living room drinking a beer while we emptied the prescription capsules. When we were finished, Frank asked us to sit with him while he drank another beer. He wanted to tell us his life story. When he finished, he stood up and asked if we minded if he smoked a cigarette. When he started toward the front door, we asked where he was going. "I never smoke in the house," he said, "I'm sure not going to start now."

When Frank came back in, he took a Dunkin' Donuts box out of the refrigerator and began making a pot of coffee. We asked if we could help. "No," he replied. "I bought the doughnuts today for you and now I want my last act on earth to be doing something nice for two wonderful people."

Frank finished making the coffee, walked into his bedroom, and said he was ready. He asked for a good-bye hug from each of us, thanked us again, and drank the medication. In less than two minutes, Frank was asleep. Two hours later we called his niece to tell her that he had died peacefully. We gave Compassion the twenty dollars he insisted we take so we could stop for dinner on our way back to Portland.

❋

For some of our clients, the help they want from Compassion is very concrete. In Maria's case, the request was tangible and specific. When she contacted Compassion she was living in a medical foster home because she could no longer care for herself.

In her thirties, Maria had lived with a malignant brain tumor for over a year. She had tried every medical treatment her doctors suggested because she wanted to fight for her life. By the time she called Compassion, her goal was to avoid prolonged dying if life no longer had meaning or purpose to her. She was interested in "the facts" about the law, but she also wanted visits. She wanted to tell her story. Compassion trains its volunteers to be active listeners because almost everyone wants or needs to tell his or her story.

Each time I leave a client I ask, "Is there anything else I can do to be helpful?" On my second visit Maria responded, "You know life is too short for the cheap toilet paper they have here. Do you think you could bring me some good toilet paper?" From then on, every time I visited, I brought toilet paper. My visits continued each week until she died in her sleep. She never pursued getting medication to hasten her death but she told me again and again that it gave her serenity to know she could.

＊

Almost all the people we work with tell us in one way or another how important it is for their peace of mind to know that they can hasten their death if their suffering becomes intolerable. For some, knowing they can get the medication is sufficient. Others need to have the medication in their possession to achieve that peace.

Charles, a man in his sixties struggling with advanced lung cancer, was one of the latter. He never wanted home visits but he was agreeable to frequent phone calls. Soon after he got his medication I called and found him to be very upbeat. "Now that I have my security stash, I've decided to live until I die," he told me. "What's going to be different for you?" I asked. "Well, for one, I bought a Corvette last Saturday and I'm going to drive the hell out of it in the time I have left." And he did. Several months later he died, never feeling the need to hasten his death.

Constance and her husband Ben wanted help explaining to their teen-age son and daughter that Constance was planning to hasten her death. She had battled brain tumors for more than ten years—over half of her children's lives. They were having difficulty recognizing their mom was getting progressively sicker. Constance had lost her ability to walk and was gradually losing her speech. She did not want to linger until all her dignity was gone.

Constance wanted to be honest with her children. She did not want them to learn years later that she had hastened her death and feel their mother had deceived them. She also did not want her husband to have to bear the burden of that secret. Constance and Ben arranged individual counseling for fifteen-year-old Tyler and seventeen-year-old Sara. Each of them walked out during their first counseling session and refused to go back.

I had been visiting the family for several months, so both children were accustomed to seeing me. Constance and Ben asked me to help them open the discussion about Constance's declining health and plan to hasten her death. The parents reasoned that I would not be as threatening as a therapist and their home would be a safer environment than a therapist's office for this discussion. At the parents' request, I made daily visits during the final weeks of Constance's life. Over several days, the parents drew Sara and Tyler into the conversation, asking first what they understood about their mother's illness and then broaching the subject of her impending death.

Perhaps because of Constance's urgency or perhaps because the conversation included me, Sara and Tyler heard the message. There were tears and difficult silences but over the course of ten days the children were able to move from denial to anger to reluctant acceptance of their mother's plan. Tyler asked his mom to wait two days so they could spend that additional time together as a family. Constance readily agreed. She and Ben were relieved that they could be open with their children and that both Tyler and Sara chose to be present at her death.

After Constance's death, both children said that even though it was the most difficult thing they had ever done, they were glad they were with their mom. They were glad to be able to give their mother one last gift of their support.

Dave, a twenty-six-year-old graduate student with a particularly virulent form of cancer wanted his mother to understand why he didn't want any more medical treatment or trips to the hospital. "I don't know if I'm going to hasten my death," he told me. "I just want my mother to understand why I might. She thinks if I accept what's happening to me and I stop fighting it means I don't love her."

I met with Dave and his mother at the inpatient hospice where he lived. I asked him to tell me the story of his illness. Over the next hour he recounted how hard he had fought and detailed all the treatments he had had including the side effects. He talked about his disappointment with each treatment failure and how difficult it was to psych himself up for the next one. In spite of everything he realized none of the treatments worked. His doctors had told him there was nothing more to be done. He also talked about how he had come to accept what was happening. Now, he was asking his mother to accept his fate, too. She listened with rapt attention.

When Dave was finished talking, I asked his mother to explain to him how hard it was for a mother to stop searching for one last miracle cure for her child. They both talked about how difficult it was to realize he wasn't going to be able to fulfill his enormous life potential. There were tears and hugs as they finally acknowledged the proverbial elephant in the living room. Dave was going to die and nothing could change that fact. Now he wanted to negotiate how it would happen. His mother listened and accepted her son's horror of going back to the hospital. They reached an understanding. Dave would not go to the hospital again and his chart at the hospice would be marked, "Do Not Resuscitate."

Soon after our meeting I spoke with Dave. He had decided not to pursue hastening his death and there was nothing more he wanted from Compassion. He said his relationship with his mother was much more relaxed and they were enjoying the time they had together. He was grateful to Compassion for facilitating the discussion and he told me he was ready to die. Six weeks later, Dave died.

※

One of the guidelines of Compassion is that it is always about the client's choice and options. We work with people to help them achieve a peaceful and dignified death, as they define it for themselves. Sometimes that means listening beyond what they're saying and hearing what they mean. Bill was a perfect case in point.

"I have two kinds of cancer and I'm tired of fighting to get doctors to take me seriously," Bill told me at our first meeting. "I just want to get my lethal medication as soon as I can because I can't go on living this way." For more than twenty minutes he outlined the futility of his life, detailing all the reasons he should be allowed to die. He finished his monologue by asking, "Why can't I just go into a nursing home and die?"

What I heard behind a very well constructed wall of anger was tremendous sadness. One of Bill's complaints was that he had to take three buses to get to a doctor's appointment and spent two hours on the bus each way. Bill had no friends or family to help him. The first three times I asked if I could take him to the doctor Bill said, "No." I kept asking and eventually he realized I meant it.

At the first doctor's appointment I went to with Bill, it became clear his anger made it difficult for him to communicate effectively with his doctors. They were dismissive and tuned Bill out as soon as he became argumentative. Bill was an extremely intelligent man. When we talked, he was open to considering that his approach wasn't getting him what he wanted—a cohesive medical plan to treat his metastatic prostate cancer.

In the following nine months, I worked with Bill to gain his trust and to diffuse his anger. I accompanied him to all his medical appointments. In the end, Bill achieved his goal. The doctors began to treat him with respect and address his complaints. They enrolled Bill in an eight-week course of radiation therapy.

All Bill's doctors were aware of the quality of life he wanted to achieve: to be sufficiently pain free to sleep through the night and to play duplicate bridge again. Most importantly, Bill felt that he was working with a medical team that cared about him and his quality of life. He said frequently, "I can live with the probability of dying but I couldn't face it when I thought none of my doctors cared. Even if I die, I'll know that I gave it a good fight."

Three Compassion volunteers shuttled him back and forth to his radiation treatment, five mornings a week for eight weeks. We also supported him through several surgical procedures to deal with side effects of the cancer and the treatment. The more rigorous the treatment, the more peaceful and calm Bill became. He often asked, "Why do you and Compassion care enough to do all of this for me?" I explained it was important to us to ensure that everyone be able to face death on their own terms. To Bill, a peaceful death was possible only if he felt he had done everything he could to survive. Finishing his course of radiation became his goal. We set up a schedule to ensure his success because, for him, that's how we could help.

Shortly after his sixty-eighth birthday Bill finished his radiation. His goal had been achieved and he was satisfied. About three weeks later he developed pneumonia. I sat with him in the hospital for three days before he died. He was a different man from the one I had met nine months earlier. Bill often said that Compassion, and the way we treated him, restored his belief that God existed.

"Compassion is God's love made manifest through angels on earth," he would say. After his initial request, he never again mentioned hastening his death. That was not the right choice for Bill.

The people with whom I have been privileged to work represent a cross-section of the population. They have been old and young, financially wealthy and just getting by, highly educated and grade school drop-outs, deeply religious and believing in nothing spiritual. What they have not been is also significant. The people I worked with have not been in uncontrollable pain, depressed, uninsured, pressured by family to end their lives, or afraid of being abandoned.

As different as these clients were, they shared a deeply held, and often long time belief that they did not want to be suspended in limbo between life and death, once their dying became inevitable. These people wanted to be able to end their dying process legally, at a time of their choosing. They made their requests to hasten death after a great deal of thought and consideration. Those who used the law did so only when they felt they could no longer go on.

All of the individuals were likable and most had wonderful senses of humor. Many were colorful characters whom I wish I could have known better. I am profoundly grateful to them for allowing me to be a part of their lives. I have received far more than I have given and I carry their wisdom with me every day.

Six

Vignettes for Living and Dying

GEORGE EIGHMEY AND TERESA GROVE

*I*n 1997, after Oregon voters approved aid in dying for the second time, Compassion in Dying formed a chapter in Oregon to bring its experience to implementation of the new law. George Eighmey and Teresa Grove came to Compassion of Oregon shortly after its formation in November 1997. They soon became devoted to guiding terminally ill patients through the legal process to access the law and making certain all underlying concerns were addressed.

George Eighmey first joined Compassion of Oregon as a board member. He followed Judith Fleming as the executive director in 1998. Prior to working with Compassion he practiced law and served six years as a representative in the Oregon legislature. No stranger to end-of-life concerns, George also served on the board of Our House of Portland, an organization operating a care facility for persons living with AIDS. George brought his legal expertise and ethic of community service to Compassion and developed a process to guarantee Oregonians a safe and humane death and serve both the spirit and the letter of the law.

Teresa Grove became Chair of the Board of Compassion of Oregon in 1999 after participating in 1998 as a volunteer. She came to the post with a long-standing interest in end-of-life care and choices. She had spent twenty years as a critical care nurse and educator, served on medical ethics committees, and conducted doctoral research in nursing ethics. In critical care she had seen far too many patients suffer painful and prolonged deaths. Teresa's experiences led her to Compassion, where she could advocate for mentally competent, terminally ill adults to have the option to die with dignity.

During their years with Compassion, George and Teresa have had the privilege of working with individuals they describe as "some of the most courageous people we have ever met." Although their clients represent a cross section of society, one common characteristic in their more than 450 clients is an abundance of love for family and friends. They find that by the time most people accept the inevitability of death they also embrace one fundamental value of this life—caring for their loved ones.

Compassion of Oregon is able to serve people throughout the state through the assistance of more than four hundred physicians, twenty-five pharmacists, and twenty-two trained client support volunteers. These individuals work daily with terminally ill individuals. They hear the life story highlights of hundreds of people. These stories illustrate the full range of human emotion—from profound tenderness to hearty laughter to thoughtful last acts—all intensified by the reality of impending death.

Teresa and George compiled the following vignettes from their own experiences and from those of other Compassion volunteers to illustrate the poignancy that can accompany a conscious end-of-life choice. They believe, and I agree, these stories bring insight, comfort and understanding to the national dialogue on aid in dying.

We have changed names to respect the privacy of the clients and their families, but in all other respects the stories are true.

※

ZACK'S PAJAMAS

While driving back to Compassion's offices from the coast on a clear summer afternoon George received a call from a woman whose husband, Zack, wished to hasten his death. He told his wife, "The quality of my life has become totally unacceptable." He was diagnosed with mesothelioma, an aggressive and painful disease generally caused by extensive exposure to asbestos. Zack received all of the recommended treatments, but to no avail.

He was enrolled in hospice and said he was receiving the best comfort care available, but he still wished to consider the option of using Oregon's law. Zack told his wife Joan that he wanted to stop his suffering immediately. Zack begged her to end his life. She told George she was going to honor his request unless we could help them that day. George assured Joan that he would come to their home immediately to talk about the process.

George and Compassion's staff nurse arrived at the couple's home within the hour. Their home was nestled in the coastal mountain range overlooking a cool stream. When Joan opened the door she was simultaneously crying and laughing, a combination of emotions that is not uncommon during a crisis. Joan was under tremendous pressure, and she was grateful for advocates to help.

For an hour the Compassion advocates explained the process to Joan and Zack, reassuring them that Zack would probably qualify to use the law since his two physicians affirmed his eligibility and were willing to participate. When they were done talking, Zack smiled and turned to his wife and said, "You are the greatest." George got up and started walking to the kitchen for a glass of water. He accidentally stepped on Zack's oxygen line, whereupon Zack grabbed his throat, let out a gurgling gasp and quipped, "So that is how you do it." Horrified, George apologized profusely. Then Zack burst into laughter, pleased with his joke. George and the nurse left shortly afterward, receiving hugs of appreciation from Joan and Zack.

On the day Zack decided he was ready to die he asked Joan, two close friends, and two Compassion volunteers to be with him. He had numerous questions for the volunteers ranging from "How does the medication taste?" to "How long will it take to drop into a coma?" He was also concerned that he might soil himself. We assured him that would not happen. Then he asked, "Can I wear what ever I want?" "Yes, of course yes," we responded.

Zack decided to wear a pair of silk pajamas Joan had given him twenty-five years earlier, still wrapped in the original package. He thought it would please his wife if he finally wore them. After putting on the pajamas Zack turned to one of the volunteers and whispered, "Now I know why I never wore these things." But the smile on Joan's face when she saw him more than compensated for any uncomfortable feelings Zack had about wearing silk PJs.

Zack asked his friends and the volunteers if they would please step into the other room while he and Joan spent some time together. He then climbed into bed. As they left the bedroom, one of the volunteers overheard Zack say to his wife, "It has been a wonderful journey. I don't regret one moment and even though I am leaving sooner than I want, I know someday you will be with me."

After a short time, Joan called everyone back into the room. She said Zack was ready. A Compassion volunteer told Zack he could change his mind at any time prior to drinking the medication. He said he was ready. Zack drank the mixture quickly and asked his wife to curl up next to him. He took her hand and said, "I love you. If there is something on the other side I will give you a sign." She held Zack gently while he quietly closed his eyes.

Within a few minutes Zack died as he wished—with dignity and grace. With tears in her eyes, Joan turned to the volunteers and said, "Thank you. You performed two wonderful deeds. You prevented Zack from committing a violent suicide and me from committing a homicide. You truly are saints."

It took Joan a long time to adjust to losing Zack, but she has learned to cope. Now, she volunteers for hospice and provides comfort to others facing a terminal illness.

DON'S CASKET FITTING

Don was in his late seventies when he learned he would not live to see his eightieth birthday. In recent years he had lost his wife, a brother, and a son. He handled the news of his impending death in the same way he handled all bad news—he faced it head-on. "My time has come," Don told Compassion workers calmly.

Organized and accepting, Don began to make certain all his final affairs were in order. He prepared his advance directive, specifically stating that he did not wish to receive life-sustaining treatment if his heart should stop. He also arranged for his funeral and wrote specific instructions on how he wanted the memorial service to go.

Only one thing troubled Don and he shared his concern with a Compassion volunteer: "Will the casket fit me?" he asked with a twinkle in his eye. The volunteer did a double take and realized it was only Don's eccentric humor at play. Playing along, the volunteer jokingly suggested that Don have his casket delivered to his home so he could try it on for size. The Compassion volunteer then moved on to other conversation and thought no more of Don's comment.

Several weeks went by while Don and his volunteer completed the process to get the medication to end his life. One day the Compassion volunteer arrived for a scheduled visit at Don's house and gave her pre-agreed "rat-ta-tat, rat-ta-tat, rat-ta-tat" knock on his front door. Usually, Don greeted her at the door with one of his jokes, sometimes off-color, but often simple and cute puns. However, this time she heard Don calling, "Come in and come out to the back patio." The volunteer feared he might be injured, so she hurriedly entered the house and rushed to the back patio.

As she headed to the patio, she caught a glimpse of a casket resting on a gurney. The sight alarmed her. But what was even more unusual was Don in the casket wriggling around a bit as he determined the fit. "You know, I think this thing is a tad too tight around my shoulders," Don said with a straight face. "I am going to have to ask the funeral guy to adjust it." Then he sat up in the casket, consumed with a laughter that shook his body from head to foot. The two laughed for a long time.

Don's wonderful, albeit odd, sense of humor was infectious. He made all those who cared for him feel good inside and out. On the day he died his loved ones and the Compassion volunteer, who by then had become one of his dearest friends, were at his side as he took the medication and said his last farewell.

HARRY'S FORT KNOX ANNEX

Harry was in his sixties when he learned of his terminal cancer. College educated, divorced, remarried, fiercely independent and spiritual, he was determined to make his death a dignified one.

When Harry married his second wife, Jean, some twenty years prior, he found in her the mate with whom he wished to spend his remaining years. His kind of love was one of the rare types—he simply could not be without his wife. They worked, traveled, and played together. Harry had no children from his first marriage, but Jean had three daughters. Together they raised the children, and the girls grew to love Harry as their father.

Harry had been healthy and active up to a week before his cancer diagnosis. His particular form of cancer caused him to deteriorate rapidly. At the point he was confined to his bed, Harry decided to call Compassion for assistance.

After several weeks, Harry's doctor was able to provide his requested prescription to end his life. On the day Harry chose to take the medication his wife and three daughters were at his side. Also present were George and another Compassion volunteer who had worked with Harry. Before taking the medication, Harry asked to be alone with Jean so he could say his final good-byes. Their daughters and the Compassion volunteers waited in the living room, visiting and sharing stories about Harry.

After an hour Harry called us into the bedroom and prepared to drink the medication at the time he had determined. He made some small talk about the weather, how it was a perfect day to die and how wonderful it was to have everyone with him. Then Harry asked for the glass of liquid. George handed it to him and told him he could change his mind if he wished. Harry simply said, "Thank you, I will take it now." He held the glass a moment, looked around at the faces of his daughters and wife, smiled softly, and then drank the liquid.

After placing the empty glass on the bedside table, Harry sat up in his bed. He hugged his wife and said, "If there were any more love in this room they would have to build an annex to Fort Knox to store it. I am a very lucky guy." He held Jean in his arms and quietly closed his eyes.

✳

ROBERT'S LIVING WAKE

Robert developed AIDS in the early 1980s when the disease was first classified as an epidemic. When he died in 2003 he was known as one of the longest survivors of the disease. Robert was an emergency medical technician and had seen numerous tragic deaths. He often said if he had complied with the wishes of all those victims who begged him to hasten their death he would be in prison for one hundred lifetimes. Although he knew he couldn't fulfill their requests, witnessing their agony convinced him that if he ever felt his life was no longer worth living, he wanted the means to hasten his death.

During his years living with AIDS Robert became somewhat of a celebrity spokesperson for the aid in dying movement. He appeared on TV, debated opponents, and campaigned for the passage of Oregon's law. When the law passed he was among the first to request assistance under it. Several times doctors told Robert he probably had only a short time to live, but he always seemed to bounce back and outlive the prognosis. Eventually, however, he acquired an aggressive form of cancer that is associated with AIDS. He knew no miracle was going to keep him going this time. His condition was quickly deteriorating. For almost two years he had postponed taking the medication to hasten his death, but now he knew the time was at hand. He called George, his support contact at Compassion, to let him know he planned to take the medication.

On the day he chose to die, Robert wanted to receive one last communion at his home. He also wanted it to be on a day when most of his family and friends could be in attendance. He chose May 3.

On that bright Saturday morning family and friends filled Robert's home, but Robert was no where to be found. George learned that Robert, known to his friends as meticulous in all details, had asked to be taken to his bank to finish one last matter. He soon returned home to a house filled with about sixty family and friends. Robert greeted each guest by name and spent at least a minute or two of private time with each person.

When he finished, it was time to begin the religious ceremony. The minister gathered the guests in the backyard around a communion table and altar. An uneasy quiet settled over the gathering as people realized they were participating in "a living wake." The minister talked about the wonderful deeds Robert had performed. Others told of how Robert had changed their lives for the better. Robert himself told the gathering how much he appreciated their love and friendship. He then invited each person to participate in the Eucharist. The wafers and wine were passed solemnly to each person who wished to partake in this symbol of life after death. After communion the minister concluded the service. Then he announced that Robert was now going to his bedroom.

The emotional atmosphere in the bedroom was heavy with grief, as well as a large dose of awe and respect for Robert's courage and his decision. Robert's family—mother, father, brother, sister, and their spouses—stood at the end of Robert's bed. His life partner sat on the edge of the bed next to Robert. Each family member had already said his or her personal good-bye.

After the minister bestowed the last rites Robert said a prayer and asked that he be accepted into God's hands. Robert's partner handed him the glass of medication. Robert drank it in less than a minute, placed his arm around his mate and said all would be okay. His partner sobbed in Robert's arms. Robert reassured all present that he would soon be in a better place. Then he closed his eyes.

While people waited in another part of the house for the announcement that Robert had died they told numerous stories about Robert's antics. Their affection filled the house with a sense of warmth and calm. Less than an hour after Robert drank his medication his twenty-year struggle with AIDS was over.

KATE CHENEY WITH HER DAUGHTER ERIKA (LEFT) GREAT GRANDSON
NICHOLAS, AND GRANDDAUGHTER HEIDI (RIGHT)

*My Grandmother was so resolved.
There was nothing about her that would
make me think this woman was being
forced into this decision.*

PAT BOWMAN
GRANDDAUGHTER

Seven

Kate Cheney

*K*ate Cheney and her family volunteered to be completely open about their experience with Oregon's aid in dying law. The first to do so, they hoped if they made their story public, it might smooth the path for others. Although confident they had no reason to be secretive, they came to understand that inviting a newspaper reporter to witness intimate details, including confidential medical records, could produce unintended consequences.

Kate, eighty-five years old, faced a terminal cancer and rapidly declining physical condition. She decided she wanted the option to take medication to hasten her death. Kate told her family she was not afraid of death, and she wanted to die in her own way. Her daughter, Erika Goldstein, and all five of her grown grandchildren supported Kate's decision. Erika, a retired nurse, and her husband, Robert, a retired teacher, were able to actively advocate for Kate. Granddaughter Pat Bowman, a social worker, and Pat's husband, Richard, a psychologist, live in Portland and were able to help as well in Kate's final months as she pursued the process to become eligible for aid in dying.

When one psychiatrist questioned Kate's competence, additional evaluations became necessary and the lengthy process began to disturb Erika. In frustration she wrote a letter to the editor of the *Oregonian* describing her experience that the law's legal safeguards were functioning more as roadblocks. A newspaper reporter seized the opportunity to chronicle the family's journey for several months, and all agreed the *Oregonian* would publish the story after Kate's death.

As expected, about six weeks after Kate died, a two-page article described the elaborate process she underwent to acquire medication under the Act. It detailed how many times Kate was obliged to demonstrate her mental competence and the voluntary and enduring nature of her request. It described how, in the end, Kate did get final approval and received her prescription. The article ended with a poignant and detailed account of Kate's final act, surrounded by a loving family.

The law's opponents used this newspaper article to manufacture controversy. Kate Cheney's family became victims of accusations and innuendoes from organizations and individuals opposed to aid in dying under any circumstance. Ugly letters, even death threats, accused Erika, Kate's physicians and others of unethical behavior. Although their charges have no foundation, opponents repeatedly label Kate's death a so-called abuse of Oregon's law. Erika and Robert endured relentless accusations for some time before deciding to leave the state.

Unfounded attacks were so pervasive that Kaiser Permanente's regional medical director, Dr. Allen Wyland, felt compelled to defend Kate Cheney, her family, and the process they underwent in a published article. "Throughout this process, the only goal of the numerous health professionals caring for Cheney was to understand and facilitate what she wanted at the end of her life." He added that critics should worry "about the impact of [their] opinions on Kate Cheney's family who gave her their love and support through a difficult final illness and the health professionals who cared for her with integrity, compassion, and the highest medical ethical standards."

Erika and Bob Goldstein, and Kate's granddaughter, Pat Bowman, share their stories about their mother and grandmother, whom they remember as "a strong and determined woman" all of her life. They were with Kate the day she chose to die.

ERIKA
Daughter, retired nurse, and mother

Over the years my mother had been ill but they didn't diagnose her cancer until she became seriously ill in April 1999. My husband, Bob, and I live in Tucson, Arizona. We were home when the doctor called us. My hearing is impaired because I had scarlet fever as a child, so I put Bob on the phone to make sure we understood everything. The doctor told Bob she had an inoperable cancerous tumor in her stomach and she had three to six months to live.

A few days later I left for Portland and by the time I arrived, my mother was already in hospice care. The last few months of my mother's life I stayed with her in her Portland home, along with her dachshund, Shorty. Later, my daughter Pat and my husband joined me.

Mom wanted to inquire about getting medication to end her life and have it available so she could take it if she chose to. We talked with her family doctor, and he said, "You are in the hands of hospice. They will keep you comfortable if your fear is pain." My mother said that was not her only fear. I think her primary fear was losing her independence. When she was about sixty-four, she had an ileostomy, which required having a bag for her stool. She had a lot of feelings about it that I do not think we ever addressed fully. One time when we were in Italy on vacation I coaxed my mother into the swimming pool at our hotel. She loved to swim, but she was afraid the bag would burst open. I said, "Mom, if anything happens I have this huge towel. I'll take care of you. Don't worry, just enjoy it." And she did. But with that ileostomy, she already had a more compromised life. The quality of her life changed.

The Kaiser Permanente Medical System requires everyone asking to use the law to be evaluated by an independent psychiatrist or psychologist. My mother was amused because there is so much therapy in this country, and yet, we never had half a minute of therapy for all the stuff we endured in Germany. We lived through the 1945 bombing of Dresden; I was only ten years old at the time. My mother was taken away by the Russians and almost raped. We were prisoners. People were blown up in front of her. There were lots of reasons for us to have had some kind of therapy, but we had absolutely no therapy. So this, coming at this point in her life, amused her.

The first psychiatrist asked Mom all these questions. She showed Mom pictures of animals, buildings, and assorted things, and then she wanted Mom to recall them. The psychiatrist asked, "When did the doctor tell you your diagnosis?" Keep in mind that my mom had fallen and was taking pain medication, and she couldn't remember small details. Her answers were sometimes halting. Then the psychiatrist said to me, "I have some questions for you, too." I said, "That's fine." I answered whatever she asked me, but I cannot recall a single question now. Finally, the doctor gave her opinion. She said to Mom, "It is my opinion that you are not capable of making the kind of decision that this procedure requires at this time, in your mental state. So I cannot grant you the permission to go ahead with this." In other words, she was saying, "You can't make a decision for yourself and your life, because you are not in your right mind."

My mother looked at her, and said, "Get out of my house. I can't believe you can tell me something like this when for over eighty years I have never asked for help from the state or government or anyone. I've never received anything. I've always taken care of myself and made decisions for myself and now you are going to tell me I don't have the capacity to do that?" She was really worked up. I was sitting there thinking, "Mom you are great. Good for you." My mother was such a role model for women. Of course, that didn't change anything. The psychiatrist, in her Birkenstocks with two smiley-face stickers on her toes, left. When she was gone my mother and I laughed. "Can you believe that?" she said. And I responded, "I can't believe it in this day and age."

This doctor had told us we could have another opinion, so we opted for that. A clinical psychologist came and I was prepared with a tape recorder, but she would not allow me to be present for the interview. She said, "I'm sorry, it is my policy never to talk to anyone else in a private interview. It is just myself and the client or patient." So I went for a walk. When I came back, she asked me a few questions, but she was fine with Mom.

This whole process with psychiatric evaluations took several weeks. In the meantime Mom was getting weaker and weaker because she was bleeding more. At any point she had the option to get more transfusions, but in her mind, transfusions would also prolong her life. She chose not to do that. She didn't want to be in the hospital at all.

There were times when my mother would turn to me and say, "Why can't they just give me that stuff, let me have it?" I would answer, "Well, I don't understand it myself." When the doctors were there in her presence she didn't have any fears, but she didn't have the energy to go out and fight, to get on the phone and ask a lot of questions. She wanted me to do the talking. Mom wanted the prescription and she wanted to have control, to make her own decision.

The two psychiatric evaluations each reached a different conclusion. Dr. Richardson [Director of the Kaiser Permanente Ethics Service] was overseeing my mom's case. He called and said, "We've got one who says yea and another says nay, so we will have to have a third one before we go any further." My daughter called him "the tie-breaker."

Dr. Richardson is an incredibly nice guy. My mom liked him right away and they had a long talk. He determined that Mom was competent and that she was acting on her own. Dr. Richardson decided she was qualified to receive the prescription. Finally, a pharmacist showed up with the medication and explained the procedure. Then I put the drugs in the closet. We didn't talk about it for a month.

I am a nurse by profession, but I also have a master's degree in women's studies. I feel strongly about women's causes and I think that my passion can come across as being maybe aggressive or super assertive. I don't know, maybe I was abrasive to some people. But I was marching for my mother, and my feeling was that I have the energy to do this on her behalf.

Before my mom got the medication, I was tired of her getting the runaround. It was proceeding slower than both of us thought it should for her to actually get this medication. After at least six weeks, maybe almost eight weeks, I wrote to the newspaper and said, "It is hard for me to understand, if there is a law that exists and is on the books, why is it so difficult to implement it? I want you to explain that to me."

That letter is what started the media attention. A newspaper reporter called me and she interviewed Mom and me both. I was impressed with her. The reporter had permission from my mom and me to do whatever she wanted with my mother's medical history and to talk with her doctors. My mom and I both agreed on this. After the reporter's article was published in the paper, I got mail telling me that I was a murderer and I was the one who should die. I may have gotten phone calls too, but I didn't always answer the phone.

If someone made accusations against me or my family now, I would say, "How can you tell me what I'm thinking? You have no right." I guess people have a right to feel the way they want to, but I say, "If you don't believe in something, don't do it." That is the way life should be, and that is what my mom said. Nobody ever helped her or doubted her ability to do anything else in her life. But in the final months of her life when she wanted to die, some wanted to question her sanity. That was a total insult to her.

The last few days of my mother's life, I moved a mattress into her bedroom and lay on the floor near her bed. I told my mom, "I want to make sure that when you get up to go to the bathroom, you won't fall and hurt yourself. Wake me up." She wouldn't do it, but she would turn all the lights on when she went to the bathroom. I would wake up, and I would watch her standing in the bathroom, emptying her bag by the toilet. One time I watched her meticulously clean out this bag where her stool came out. Then she put the clip back on. I would venture to say she was in the bathroom at least thirty minutes. I felt sad because it seemed like this was the last small piece of control she had in her life. This just really saddened me.

Then one day Mom said, "I think this is the day." So I called my daughter, Pat, and she and her husband Richard came over. They sat on Mom's bed and asked her if this is what she really wanted. Then Pat called the other grandchildren and they cried as each one talked with his or her grandmother.

Mom thought of her five grandchildren—Pat, Ernie, Kathy, Nicole, and Heidi—as "perfect." I used to tease her and ask, "Do you have any perfect children?" Of course, meaning *me!* We would laugh and she would keep talking about her perfect grandhcildren.

In the kitchen we all worked together to mix the medicine in a bowl of applesauce. Mom ate it all, and then we all had a glass of wine, Liebfraumilch, and toasted her, which was what she wanted. She took a sip. I remember telling her in German that I appreciated what a tough old lady she was. Then she corrected my German.

Looking back now, I think it is wonderful that this law is in effect. The fact that I got involved in trying to make it more efficient for my mom might have been my own character. I believe the process itself went very well. They have to have all those safeguards in place to protect people. The process took a long time, but it worked well. All the safeguards are there. I cannot see how anybody can question it.

PAT BOWMAN
granddaughter, and social worker who works in child welfare

I went to visit my grandmother at a Catholic hospital after her diagnosis. The nurse came to me and said, "She is asking the doctor for medication. Can you talk to her?" My grandmother said, "I don't want it to be like this, I'm scared of lingering and I want to be in control." I told her, "We can talk about that." I went to the nurse and asked if there was anybody who would talk to Kate or me about assisted suicide. The nurse just looked at me and said, "There is a law, but it is not a law that anybody is going to help you with here. This is a Catholic hospital. We can't even discuss this with you." So Kate was moved to Kaiser hospice care.

As my mother described, Kate was repeatedly assessed to determine if she was mentally capable of choosing physician-assisted death. At one point, I remember Grandma saying, "They want to know if I'm crazy." One day we were talking about her going to yet another mental evaluation, and I said, "Who is the president?" She answered, "Nixon, I know that…. Ha! Just jiving." She had an incredible sense of humor about it all.

During the evaluations she just didn't remember details. One of the doctors focused on things she was not going to remember. "When was the Gulf War? When did you first find out about X, Y, or Z?" She was not that linear. And one doctor decided she wasn't competent because of that. But my grandmother always was steadfast about not wanting to lose her quality of life and independence and her ability to do things she had done before.

My grandmother was so resolved. There was nothing about her that would make me think this woman was being forced into this decision. Yeah, maybe her body was forcing her. But she was very clear. When she died my husband, Richard, a psychologist, propped her up while she ate the applesauce. We were all around her. Then she just closed her eyes, and that was it.

BOB GOLDSTEIN
Son-in-law, teacher of history and English

Katie had said that if she couldn't live the kind of life she was accustomed to, she didn't want to go on any longer. In my opinion, that was perfectly consistent with her behavior because my memories of Katie are very vivid. She was a vigorous woman who walked her dog every day, went swimming, liked to be outdoors working in her garden, liked to read, and played the piano. She was always engaged in a number of activities. She was eighty-five when she got the terminal diagnosis. Katie felt her life had been full, and she was ready for it to end.

Those last days with Katie were great. I walked with her and the dog and we just talked. Katie was a lovely woman. She liked books and music, a nice bottle of wine at dinner, and the kinds of things that I liked. She had a great sense of humor. It was a lot of fun and a joy for me to be around her. I was happy to be there, not only to support Erika but to be with Katie.

I am not a person who engages other people easily, but I had no reservations about Katie. I knew her about sixteen years and I liked her right from the start. She had a zest for living. We could talk seriously about things, but we could laugh and joke as well.

I don't think Erika ever lost her focus to support her mother's decision. The hospice social worker, Elise, was remarkably understanding, compassionate, and open. She was so skillful in her relationship with Katie and her family. Elise had all of the skills required to help Katie through this process. I can't speak highly enough of her.

I have always felt we have a right to make choices about how we want to live, and we also ought to have the right to choose how we die. In this case it was very clear to me that Katie knew exactly what she wanted to do, and her request had to be honored. It was in keeping with the dignity and integrity of this person.

RICHARD HOLMES

As sick as he was, and although
he was getting weaker by the day,
he was still fun to be around
and even funny.
My dad knew, till the end,
how to enjoy life.

RICK HOLMES, SON

Eight

Richard Holmes

More than once Richard Holmes opted for heroic medical measures to save his life. In 1995 he underwent heart surgery and in 1996 he received a liver transplant. He was determined to beat the odds again in 2000 when doctors diagnosed colon cancer. He underwent surgery and a lengthy, intense course of chemotherapy. It looked as though he had won when doctors declared Richard cancer free in 2001. However, in a short time the cancer had spread to Richard's liver and was inoperable. His doctor told him he had about six months to live.

A gregarious, life-loving man, Richard did not want to die a solitary or violent death; nor did he want to spend his last days in the fog that painkillers can induce. Until the end, he wanted to be able to talk to his children and grandchildren. For Richard, the thought of living the last days of his life not knowing whom he was talking to or even if it were day or night was "a bad legacy to leave."

Like many who consider aid in dying, Richard was determined to have some control over how he spent his last days. A retired salesman with a strong independent streak, he reasoned, "I've lived life pretty much as I've wanted to and I feel I should be able to end it if I need to."

After a fifteen-day waiting period, Richard planned to get his prescription filled on November 9, 2001. But on November 6, 2001 Attorney General John Ashcroft declared that any Oregon doctor prescribing medication for aid in dying would be breaking federal law. Stopped two days short of obtaining his prescription, Richard was Compassion in Dying's first patient plaintiff in the lawsuit, *Oregon v. Ashcroft*. Overnight he became a central figure in the legal battle. On November 8, 2001 the *Oregonian* ran Richard's picture on the front page with the headline "Ailing Man Caught in Legal Limbo."

Richard captivated the media with his common sense, humor, and courage in facing death. During a press conference he told thirty journalists, "I want the option. I want the choice—that's all I want. When the quality of my life is not worth living, then I want to stop living.... It should be my decision. I have lived my life the way I want to; I should die the way I want to. I personally think it [legal aid in dying] should be a law in every state in the whole country."

The *New York Times* published an article on Richard and Oregon's law, including his words: "It may be against his [Ashcroft's] religion but it's not against my religion. My God wouldn't tell me that I can't do this. My God would tell me it's okay to do something that's going to relieve suffering and pain.... I could do myself in in a lot of other ways. I've got three guns in the house, but that's too violent. It's too scary."

In the final months of his life Richard showed dying patients their concerns and wishes could be heard and valued. Richard put a human face on a complex legal issue. Reporters deluged Compassion with requests to speak with Richard. Knowing that every interview he gave could be his last, Richard agreed to speak with reporters from numerous media sources, including CNN, CBS News, and National Public Radio. *People* magazine featured Richard in a six-page article. After that, each time a reporter visited Richard's home he proudly showed them "The Sexiest Man Alive" issue of *People,* which also happened to include his profile.

On November 8, 2001, a federal judge in Portland issued a temporary restraining order against Ashcroft's Directive, and on April 18, 2002 he ordered the Directive permanently enjoined. These orders allowed Richard to obtain his prescription under the law. Richard and his daughter, Sandy, attended the victory press conference. Richard lived several months beyond doctors' predictions, and his daughter believes this was because he was so passionately involved with Compassion's fight to keep aid in dying legal. He died in his home September 9, 2002, but he did not use the medication he had fought so hard to obtain. All along he had said that he might never take the medicine, but he wanted the choice. He was 73 years old.

Shortly after Richard's death his grown children, Sandy and Richard, issued a statement in honor of their father: "There are two key issues that our dad tried to express. One is the comfort he felt in knowing he had the choice. He openly admitted that he didn't know if he could actually bring himself to take the prescribed medication, but it would have been unbearable to face the end drawing near without knowing the choice was his. The second point Dad felt strongly about was the rights of Oregon voters being upheld. 'What's the point!' he would say, "if the majority of the voters of this or any measure didn't have a voice." If he were here today, he'd tell Ashcroft to "Give up. You lost. Stop wasting our money."

The following stories are by Richard's children.

SANDY HOLMES
Daughter, and mother of two

"Kelly's Poolroom, Bar and Grill!"

That's how my dad would answer the phone when we were kids. He had a great sense of humor, a sense of fun that he never lost. I was clearing out his house and there on the back of his bedroom door was a poster of a young, bikini-clad model—that was so typical of him. For years he wore a belt buckle that had the inscription "God's gift to women." My dad used to insist that his hospice nurses were young and cute. He wanted to date his hospice nurse, though of course she was in her twenties and he was over seventy! It makes me laugh just to think about it.

We grew up listening to a lot of music, especially jazz, and Sinatra—my dad's musical tastes were broad as were his tastes in movies. His favorites were epic war movies, and four nights before he died my brother and Dad watched a movie together.

My dad could also be serious. As soon as he found out he had cancer he wanted to start chemo. My brother and I were with him and we tried to talk him into taking a trip with us first, but he was firm in what he wanted and he started chemo the next day. Right away he knew he wanted to fight the cancer. He had an operation to remove part of his colon, and as part of his treatment he had chemo pumped directly into him twenty-four hours a day for two weeks. That was really tough on him, but he carried on with it and ended up beating the odds. After his treatment he was declared cancer free, but when he went back for a check-up a month later they found spots on his liver. His body had turned against him and there were tumors the size of golf balls on his liver. It was inoperable.

I think timing had a lot to do with my dad being the poster child for Compassion in Dying. He had found out about the law—my uncle, who's a retired anesthesiologist, had known about it. My dad had been complying with the requirements of the law and it was just two days before he got his prescription when Ashcroft issued his Directive. My dad couldn't believe that Ashcroft got involved. He just couldn't understand why the man didn't focus on bigger issues in the country; there was certainly plenty after September 11 for Ashcroft to get involved with. He kept asking me why Ashcroft was interfering but I had no idea.

My dad wanted to speak up. It was in his nature to want to be in control. All his life he liked being in the driver's seat. I guess that it didn't really surprise me that he chose to speak up for the Death with Dignity Act. It was real obvious that speaking up made him happy. I remember him saying that he did it because he believed that if saying something helped one other person, someone who was also ill and needed the drugs, than he'd do whatever he could. I'm really proud of him for that. Wanting to help others was his main reason for coming forward.

Of course it wasn't just timing that made Dad so good at being the face for Compassion. Two other things made him a natural: he had been a Portland Rose Prince, and he had been a child actor. I am sure that's why the attention that Ashcroft's Directive brought didn't faze him. He wasn't at all bothered by the cameras. All those questions, everybody listening to him, watching him—he wasn't cowed by any of it. I went to one of his press conferences and I'm really glad I did because I got to see him in action. It really surprised me to see my dad so completely in command with everyone focused on him. The camera loved him, and he loved all the attention.

Saturday, he had been shopping and was feeling okay. But by Sunday morning we had to take him to the hospital because he started bleeding and throwing up blood. This had happened before, but he always bounced back. So, I don't think he thought he was going to die soon. I spent the day with him at the hospital, watching closely to be sure he was comfortable and pain free. It was important to me that someone was with him at all times. At the end of the day the hospital released him and said he could go home.

Once Dad was comfortable and resting in bed, my brother and I decided to trade off staying with him to be sure he was all right. I was going home to take care of my children, get some sleep, and be ready for the next day's shift. But before I left I asked my dad if it was okay to leave. He was coherent and talking when he answered, "Yes." Then he said, "Goodnight, sweetie-pie," which is what he always said. Everyone thought he would make it through the night—my brother, my uncle, and even the hospital. So I left thinking I would see him in the morning.

Later—I don't remember what time it was—my brother phoned me and said to come over, Dad was really bad. By the time I got there he had already died. He died before I had even left my house but my brother didn't want to tell me that in case I had an accident while driving to the house. My dad's kidneys had shut down by then. I think the hospital sent him home to die. He'd been asking where everyone in the family was, so I think he had a sense he was going to die. I'm just so glad there was no pain, no horrible lingering. That would have been awful for him.

I cannot say for sure, even now, if my dad would ever have taken the medication. I never really asked him and I don't think my brother did either. When my dad did talk about it, which wasn't often, he would always say, "We'll cross that bridge when we come to it." I wanted to be there when he died, even if he decided to die by taking the medication. I supported him, and so did my brother. We didn't broach the subject with him because we felt it was up to him to approach us to say what he wanted to do and to ask if he needed us. He was coherent on his last night and was able to drink on his own, so if he thought he was going to make it through the night, there was no need for any of us to get the medication for him. He never asked. My brother told me that Dad had told the nurses earlier that day that if it was his time then he was ready.

My dad wanted physician-assisted suicide to be legal in every state. I'm certain he was comforted just knowing he had the drugs. I can remember the day he got the prescription filled. We talked on the phone that day and I could just hear the change in his voice. He felt much more in control. He knew that he had power over his life again, and after all he'd been through, it was exactly what he needed. He had worked very hard to get those drugs. My dad had a total love of life, so in a way I'd have been surprised if he had taken the medication. I think he would have had to be in pain or near death for a long time before actually getting to the point of swallowing the medication.

We had the wake at O'Connors, where my dad loved to go. Since we had our New Year's Eve party there he thought it would be fun to have the wake there, too. The place was packed. He had a lot of friends, so I wasn't really surprised at how crowded it was. Everyone who knew him knew how much he cared about his friends, how he'd do anything for them. For his wake I made a three-panel display board that was about four feet tall. On this board where I'd written in big letters "Son," "Father," "Grandfather," and "Hero," I also put "Friend." Then, under all those labels I put pictures of everyone who had played a role in that part of his life. I think my dad would have really liked it.

People often want to know what my dad's religion was, if that had anything to do with his decision or if it was something he struggled with. I'm not sure what his religion was. He went to the University of Portland for a while, which is Catholic, but he didn't identify himself with any one religion. His religion was simple: to treat others as he wanted them to treat him. He didn't feel he needed to go to church to have a relationship with God.

My dad didn't leave any last words. He didn't leave any message that he wanted to go on after him. When I watch tapes of those news conferences that included my dad, I can see how special he was. I can honestly say that I remember my dad as fun and warm with a great sense of humor. He'll always be special to those who were lucky enough to know him. And I'm convinced his voice will be heard because of what he stood up for, what he spent his last days speaking out about—they were matters of freedom and compassion, and those things mattered very much to him.

RICK HOLMES
Son, physician assistant, and father of two

What I remember most about my dad was his devotion to enjoying life in his own way. He was seemingly unconcerned about how others felt about him; he did everything his own way and in his own time. He was joyfully irreverent.

He was quite a practical joker and would take great joy in scaring someone by jumping out from behind a door or grabbing them when they least expected it. One day when I was about five, my dad and I were playing hide and seek. I remember him leaping out from behind a counter to scare me. I ran straight into a wall and lacerated my forehead! He also used to take great pride in defeating every willing man (they were usually younger than him) in a foot race with a lit cigarette in his mouth throughout the sprint! When I was older and away in the navy, my friends, all obviously younger than my dad, would stop by the house just to see him. As one of my closest friends who knew my father well recently put it, "He was really a cool guy."

My dad was successful at anything he chose whether through persuasiveness or perseverance. Although that made him difficult for me to deal with sometimes while I was growing up, I now realize that these are fine qualities, and I endeavor to teach them to my own children. When I was young, he taught me in a firm yet concerned and loving way that being a man meant that I could never lie or steal and that I must treat others as I would want to be treated. He tried to live that way himself. When his parents were ill he did his best to care for them, and at one time they both lived with him. Although he found he really didn't have the skills to properly care for them, he hated having to place them in extended-care facilities. I remember him telling me when he was about fifty that he would never be put in one of those places. "I want to go at home," he said.

My father led the family through several hardships, including business failures and long-distance relocations that would try any person's mettle. He reinvented himself a couple of times in his younger days, yet all the time kept hold of his strong inner belief that life was to be enjoyed. While I was growing up he always listened to music, and I can still picture him humming or singing his Frank Sinatra songs.

Despite his serious illnesses, my dad always rallied and conquered…until the last week. On his final morning he called my house and asked me to come over because he needed help. When I got there he was standing over the sink and vomiting blood. He told me he had been sick for hours. Essentially, I took him to work with me since I worked in the emergency department, which is where he spent his last day. He called me to the bedside and asked me to make sure everyone in the family was nearby or coming.

I felt he knew he was not going to live much longer because at one point he asked me, "What do you think, did I buy the farm this time or what?" I was optimistic that he would live another day or two. I called my children and they immediately came to Portland, arriving at about two in the morning. After receiving some bedside care and medication for the nausea, he looked as though he had settled down to sleep. Later that night he called my name and I went up to his room. He looked gravely ill. I held his hands as he gasped his last breath, but I could not convince myself that he had died so I ran and got my stethoscope. I kept listening, hoping to hear something, hoping I was wrong. My children came upstairs too and we all held his hands for a long time. Even then I listened again, thinking that maybe the nausea medication had caused his shallow breathing.

To this day I am angry and indignant at how this cancer devastated such a vibrant and wonderful man. He did not choose to die this way but was determined that if this was going to happen to him, he would have the medication to end his suffering. Fortunately he did not suffer or linger in pain.

When I think of the last days I spent with him, I am strengthened by the memory of the two of us watching movies together, him telling me stories of his younger days. As sick as he was, and although he was getting weaker by the day, he was still fun to be around and even funny. My dad knew, till the end, how to enjoy life.

JAKE HARRIS

What I would like to leave is a legacy of community.
I want everybody to take heart,
to believe that you have community too.
Keep the faith, and I thank everyone involved
for making me one happy man.
I'll be waitin' for ya.

—JAKE

Nine

Jake Harris

Jake Harris was fifty-five years old when doctors told him that the melanoma on his arm had metastasized to his brain and there was no hope for a cure. At the time, Jake was living a simple life in a yurt in Eugene, Oregon. His family included a network of friends in Eugene, a grown son in Boston, and a brother in New York.

Jake lived a full and diverse life filled with numerous interests and adventures. Jake's first career as a plumber ended when he developed back problems. He then became a licensed massage therapist, and worked until he got carpal tunnel syndrome. Jake and his brother self-published a book entitled *Tales from the Plumbing Zone,* which teaches plumbing through on-the-job stories. His second book, *Anyone Can Ride a Bike,* chronicled his cross-country bike trip with his son. He bought and restored an old sailboat, then wrote about his sailing adventures with his son around the Puget Sound. In addition to being an adventurer and travel writer, Jake was a song-writer and blues musician, playing harmonica, drums, keyboard, and guitar. A long-time friend, Susi Klare, wrote about Jake's final months, and Compassion volunteer Michaele Houston shared her experiences advocating for Jake.

SUSI KLARE
A friend to Jake Harris from the mid-1970s until his death. Susi is a writer who lives in the coast range of Oregon with her husband.

THE DEATH HE WANTED

Jake's voice came through our answering machine without a trace of the usual Jake jive. The message was to cancel his fifty-fifth birthday party and to tell my husband the men's group couldn't meet in Jake's yurt. Jake's voice was as lowdown as I had ever heard it. I called him right back.

"Oh man, this is too heavy," he said. "I can't use my arm. I got a bad feeling about this."

"Is there anything I can do?" I asked. And because it was Jake and because Jake often complained that no one cared about him, I added, "I mean it, Jake. I'll come into town. You call if there's anything."

The next call came from the hospital. "Sus, they did a brain scan, they want to keep me here, they say I could get totally paralyzed any minute. No way, man, no way. I won't let them cut me again." He sounded paranoid and panicked. Before I could say anything, Jake said he had to go and abruptly hung up.

An hour or so later he called back. "I made it home," he said. "Man it feels good to be safe in my yurt." Jake had a wooden yurt tucked in the shadows of a tangled yard. One round room with a tiny bathroom attached, a space cramped with clutter—piano, keyboard, guitar, congas, his ongoing writing projects.

"This body's a junker," Jake said. "Not worth fixing any more." His voice was gentle, as if tenderized by the nearness of death. The final diagnoses wasn't in yet—the MRI showed lesions on the brain—but in light of the melanoma removed from Jake's arm one and a half years ago, I think we both knew the cancer had spread to his brain. And it wasn't just cancer. Twelve years earlier there had been back surgery and still his back went out regularly. He would lie in bed for days, nothing to do but wait out the pain. Across the round baldness of his head there was one long scar, a string of white stitches. Five years ago he'd had brain surgery to drain an infection. Then came a seizure and epilepsy, glaucoma, carpal tunnel, severe neck problems…the list goes on.

"I'll go to the forest to die," Jake said, "I'll stop eating."

This was a heavy-set man with a bad back who had pedaled a bicycle from Eugene to New York following hemorrhoid surgery. Jake did what he set out to do. I pressed the phone to my ear and pictured what Jake was saying. I saw him crawling on thick forest moss. Jake in a lovely green uncaring world. I thought of rain, mosquitoes, and cold nights, but not cold enough. Hypothermia's not the worst way to go, I thought, but it was almost June.

"I don't know, Jake," I said. "Sounds like a bad idea. It takes an awfully long time to starve to death." The diagnosis was in. As his oncologist put it, brain cancer can take the form of either meatballs or sauce. Meatballs are operable. Jake had sauce.

"Was it real, Sus?" Jake said over the phone. "Your offer to help?" He asked me to find out how he could end his life before it became intolerable. Already he was losing the use of one leg.

"It's the choice I'd make for myself," I said. "I support your decision."

I called Jake's doctor who referred me to Compassion in Dying. The director explained Oregon's Death with Dignity Act. Jake could request a prescription for a lethal dose of barbiturates as long as his decision wasn't based on depression, inadequate care, or inadequate efforts to control pain. Two doctors would have to agree on a terminal diagnosis of less than six months. They'd need to verify he was of sound mind, his decision voluntary and rational. I called Jake back to explain the law as best I could. The protocol had plenty of safeguards to prevent abuse of the act, which made for some confusing details.

I would help Jake jump through the hoops.

The women—friends and lovers from his past and present—cleaned the yurt. They cleared out the clutter and rearranged what was left of Jake's life. The men hauled off the piano and built a wheelchair ramp. They repaired the path to the driveway and fixed the rough spots where a frost-heaved brick could lurch Jake out of his wheelchair.

I drove the thirty miles from my home to Eugene. I walked up the new ramp. The railings had flower boxes. Shafts of evening sun lit the petals and led through the screen door into Jake's yurt. Inside was completely different from how I'd last seen it. Opposite the door, a hospital bed; to the left a futon couch; to the right Jake's small desk and computer. Everything was clean and organized. Jake sat in an upholstered armchair and I sat in the wheelchair.

"Wow," I said, looking around. "Nice cleanup."

"Yeah," Jake said. "The women have finally got me where they want me." Jake had a new laugh, it was kind and self-mocking. "This is good," Jake said. "This is blowing my mind." His brown eyes were wet, magnified behind the lenses of his thick glasses.

Jake didn't have a primary caregiver but he had friends who were willing to do what had to be done so he could stay home. One friend scheduled caregiver shifts, another taught us how to move Jake without injuring ourselves. Some friends gave Jake spiritual and emotional counseling, while others dealt with insurance, finances, shopping. There were over a dozen of us who coalesced into what came to be called the "Jakezone."

With so many of us sharing responsibilities, it was not that hard to fit caring for Jake into our lives. And then, as if by magic, caring for Jake became a big thing in our lives. The big thing. Jake's yurt was the place to be. It felt holy, it was a temple. Everyone felt it. Each person in the Jakezone has a story.

"We gotta move on this, Sus." Jake was on the phone telling me about going out to eat with his son Jeremy. Jeremy had flown to Eugene from Boston for the second time since this had all started less than a month ago. They had gone to New Day Bakery for breakfast, but Jake couldn't eat. He got the food on his fork, he could even lift the fork, but then something short-circuited and the food didn't make it into his mouth. Jake laughed when he told me the story, but I could tell he was worried.

Not about dying. I'd known Jake for more than twenty years, and he appeared more at peace about the reality of his death than I had ever known him to be about the reality of his life. What Jake feared was that his body would live on after he was gone. Or even worse, that he should be trapped alive inside it.

By law, Jake had to be able to drink and swallow on his own. His motor skills were dissolving and his cognitive abilities were showing signs of slippage. With parts of his brain blinking off, Jake was worried he might not have enough time left to create his own ending.

We were waiting for a doctor to make a decision. The doctors all agreed that Jake met the legal requirements for a hastened death, but getting two doctors to sign the paperwork wasn't easy. Jake's oncologist would sign, but he wouldn't prescribe. The doctors were afraid of repercussions. They wanted anonymity. I called the doctor we had been waiting to hear from, the one we were counting on to prescribe. I said we needed to see him right away. I wheeled Jake into the clinic. A nurse wanted to weigh him and take his blood pressure. I told her no, there was no need for that. The doctor came in and tried to explain how writing the prescription could be a risk to his practice. The doctor said he was sorry.

The examination room had no windows. It was a small space for three people to breathe in and out. A small room for such a huge amount of disappointment and sadness, such a weight of silence. Finally, the doctor said, "Okay, I'll do it." He had tears in eyes as he began the paperwork.

Back in the Jakezone, we taught one another how to get him out of the wheelchair and walk him to the toilet. The wheelchair didn't fit through the bathroom door. We had to be sure Jake had both feet below his knees before he tried to stand. I had to hold onto the belt around his waist, and make sure he used his left foot first when he went down the step into the bathroom. Another friend, Lela, showed me how she walked Jake. "You slip your left foot under Jake's right foot and then your leg becomes his," explained Lela. I loved how it felt to walk Jake this way. It was like a game kids would play together, but it felt even better than that.

The cancer grew and Jake got weary. As grateful as he was for the care and love he was getting, he had had enough. He asked people to stop dropping by; he didn't want phone calls. Jake was ready to get out of his body. I got the call that Jake wanted me to come. I called his Compassion in Dying caseworker in Portland and told her it could be soon now. Throughout the past month, Compassion caseworkers had helped us understand the Death with Dignity Act. They would come to support Jake and whoever was with him at the end.

Lela was in the yurt when I got there. A quiet summer evening, the next day was Independence Day, the Fourth of July. Lela asked Jake who he wanted with him when he took the pills. Jake wagged his head back and forth the way he did when he felt overwhelmed.

"Jeremy," he said. "I just want Jeremy."

Jake's chin fell to his chest and he started to cry. We touched his arms. Lela rested her hand on his knee. Then Jake named his brother in New York, who, like Jeremy, had been flying to Eugene whenever he could. Jake mentioned his ex-wife. He started naming us all—all the ones who had been his caregivers over the past month. You could hear it in his voice when he named someone, how he was remembering that person, maybe some moment between them. Finally, he just shook his head again, and said, "Jeremy."

That night Lela and I slept on the futon with Jake between us. I don't think anyone really slept. I cuddled as close as I could. It felt good to be touching Jake like that, and I felt sad when sometime in the middle of the night he asked to be moved to his hospital bed. I fell asleep next to Lela and woke up once when he called my name. He knew what he wanted but couldn't tell me. We played twenty questions until I got that it was pain pills and which ones.

My shift was over at ten the next morning. I said, "I'll come if you want me for anything else." It felt like my job was finished, like I had done all I could for Jake. Still, it was hard to leave the yurt.

I said good-bye.

The rest of what happened comes from the stories of others. His son Jeremy was in the yurt, fresh off the airplane, and so was Jake's brother. It was six in the evening when the two caseworkers from Compassion in Dying arrived from Portland. At 6:30 Jake took his anti-nausea medication so he wouldn't throw up the Seconal, which has a bitter taste that is difficult to disguise.

Jake's friends from Eugene gathered together by the Willamette River, a short distance from the yurt. Someone had a cell phone to receive the call when Jake was gone. They all sat on the ground and held vigil in a large circle. They shared stories and songs, prayers and silence. A duck took flight into the evening sun. The phone call came. Jake was pronounced dead at 7:20 p.m. on July 5, 2000.

He got the death he wanted.

MICHAELE WILK HOUSTON
Michaele attended the death of Jake Harris as a Compassion volunteer. This is her story of Jake's death.

Jake was the epitome of the adage, "People die the way they live." He lived life on his terms and he was determined to die in a manner and at the time of his choosing. Like all the other people I have worked with as a Compassion volunteer, he did not want to die. He was angry that circumstances found him in a failing body with a terminal disease that would, ready or not, take his life at age fifty-six. That anger flared up occasionally, but by the time he contacted Compassion he had pretty much accepted what he could not control. His primary concern was to insure that he could exercise his legal right to hasten his death if and when he felt his life no longer had any meaning and dignity.

Jake just wanted the facts. Unlike many people who contact Compassion, he did not want emotional support. He did not want assistance with any end-of-life issues. He did not want what he called "hand holding." He wanted guidance through the legal and medical system to guarantee that he could get the medication that would provide the option to hasten his death. Beyond that, he was willing to have Compassion volunteers present at his death to be certain the process went smoothly and to support family members who would be present.

With those caveats in place, Jake and I started having regular phone conversations. At first he was just interested in being certain he was following the required procedures. Eventually, his curiosity got the best of him; he began to talk about himself and to ask questions about me. We discovered we were age contemporaries and we had both grown up in New York. That allowed him to tease me about not sounding like I came from Brooklyn. Jake enjoyed teasing.

On good days he told me stories about his family and his experiences growing up in a middle class Jewish family in the 1950s. His sense of humor was self-deprecating, ironic, dark, and ever present.

Our phone contacts diminished over the last two weeks of his life as he grew weaker. With Jake's permission, I began to talk with Susi, one of the group of remarkable friends who physically cared for Jake and who comprised his support system. One day she called and said, "Jake is planning to take his pills tomorrow. Can you be here at 6:00 p.m.?"

I called Jake, assured him that I would come, and arranged for another Compassion volunteer who lives in Eugene to meet me at Jake's house. Compassion always asks two volunteers to be present at a hastened death for several reasons: two people can more easily divide their attentions to support both the person hastening his/her death and the family members and friends who are present. We're also able to support each other as we share in a powerful and often sacred time in a family's life.

The two-hour drive to Eugene allowed me to think about what I was about to experience. Jake was my first hastened death. Although I had been trained and I knew what to expect, I was still grateful that Justine, a more experienced volunteer, would be present.

When we arrived at Jake's we found him sitting in his chair, which he described as his "throne." He was calm, peaceful, very much in control and most surprising to me, celebratory. He had already said good-bye to his support group the previous weekend when they had crowded into a friend's home to have "a living wake" at which he was roasted and toasted.

From the instant we walked in, Jake was in charge. We introduced ourselves to him, his son Jeremy, and Jake's brother. We started to make small talk when Jake intervened. "Let's get this show on the road," he said, handing me the bottle of pills. "The kitchen is in there," gesturing to the tiny, closet-sized, room that served as the kitchen/bathroom in his yurt.

Justine and I began separating capsules and shaking out the powder which, when mixed with water, would provide Jake the peaceful and dignified exit he had chosen. Jake continued to chat with his brother and son. They were nervous but Jake was serene. We could hear the conversation, stories, and remembrances of good times. My most vivid recollection is the good nature—gentle chuckling, giggling, hearty laughter, groaning at bad jokes. The atmosphere was infused with love and peace as tangibly as the yurt was filled with light and flowers.

As Justine and I continued to empty the capsules, making a bigger and bigger pile of powder, Jake would shout periodically, "Hey, how ya doing?" Then he would make another bad joke about how upset he would be if we started sneezing.

I don't know what I expected, certainly more solemnity and seriousness—tears maybe. The gift Jake gave was to teach us to suspend any expectations and just be open to the way events unfold. Jake relied on his humor all of his life. Why would he abandon it at his death?

Justine and I finished our task. Jake would now have to wait an hour while the anti-nausea medication took effect. He asked us to wait outside and come back in exactly one hour. On our way out he looked at me quizzically, "Are you Jewish?" I could tell he was replaying our many telephone conversations and the clues I had given him. "So, you finally figured that out," I replied. Without missing a beat he rolled his eyes, looked at his brother and son and said, "I asked for the Angel of Death and they send me a Jew from Brooklyn." They were moderately horrified, but his brother was able to choke out, "That's Jake."

While we waited in the yard, we heard guitar music and singing and more laughter coming from the yurt. At the end of the hour Jake was ready. He had already said his good-byes and was now task oriented. We explained again what was going to happen. He didn't have any questions but he did have a twinkle in his eye.

"Today is a good day to die," he said gravely. He couldn't keep a straight face. "I heard that once in a movie and I've always wanted to say it."

Some people choose to have a shot of liquor after they drink the barbiturates. Jake had a pint of Southern Comfort at the ready. He thanked Jeremy and his brother for their lives and for their presence, thanked us for our help, settled back into his "throne" and drank down the liquid. He took a drink from the pint bottle, passed it to his brother who passed it to his son, each of them drinking. They passed it back to Jake and he drank again. About two minutes later, he asked, "Are you sure this is going to work?" By the time we reassured him that it would, he was asleep. His son began to sing and play the guitar and continued playing for twenty minutes until Jake's brother noticed that he had stopped breathing. Both expressed great surprise that Jake's face was at peace. The pain that they had seen for so long was gone.

As Justine and I walked out of the yurt, we were met by a phalanx of people lining the driveway and spilling out onto the road. Each was holding a lit candle; some were chanting, and all were waiting for news of Jake's departure. They had come to support Jake's family and each other, and to celebrate his life and their connection to it. It was an extraordinary tribute. Driving home, I was filled with a feeling of, "God's in His heaven, all's right with the world" as well as gratitude for having been allowed to be a part of something that brought peace to Jake, his family, and his friends.

Just before he died, Jake Harris wrote down some of his final thoughts. They appeared on a card at his memorial service.

A MESSAGE ABOUT COMMUNITY

I will start with my primal issue, feeling unloved. What the last month of my life has done for me is to allow me to believe. It showed me that, in spite of doubt, there really is Community. We have Community! Before this, it was questionable—who were we? A mere sixteen days later [after the discovery of his illness], I would have been on my motorcycle trip—alone, without all the love that has been here. Without all of you. Everyone has been incredible, with such sweet devotion I could hardly believe it. People have been so there, so present, that it got me past the embarrassment of needing so much help. It became so real that I was able to truly believe that I am loved, I am LOVE.

What I would like to leave is a legacy of Community. I want everybody to take heart, to believe that you have Community too. I think that's what I did, bringing it out of the closet. It was always here, but we didn't know the extent of the support. I was just the catalyst who brought forth our profound caring for each other. I feel so honored to be the focus of this manifestation, and I hope that you will all believe. Keep the faith, and I thank everyone involved for making me one happy man.

I'll be waitin' for ya.

—JAKE

Ten

Spiritual Perspectives for
Aid in Dying

RABBI JOSHUA STAMPFER AND REVEREND DR. PATRICIA ROSS

Rabbi Joshua Stampfer is a deeply loved and highly respected elder in the Oregon Jewish community and in the larger religious and secular communities. He was born in Jerusalem in 1921 and his family moved to the United States when he was two years old. After graduating from the University of Chicago he followed in his father's footsteps and took up rabbinical studies.

While serving congregations in Nebraska, Oregon, and Jerusalem, Rabbi Stampfer has devoted himself to international Jewish relations and the struggle for peace in the Middle East. He is a director of the World Council of Jewish Service and founder of many interfaith and international organizations working for peace and understanding throughout the world. His special interest has been the ancient Jewish communities of China and Portugal.

Rabbi Stampfer led Congregation Neveh Shalom in Portland for forty years. Neveh Shalom is the second oldest Jewish congregation in the Pacific Northwest and the oldest Conservative congregation on the West Coast. Although he moved to an emeritus position in 1993, he is still active in the life of the congregation. Rabbi Stampfer and his wife Goldie have five children and twenty grandchildren.

Rabbi Stampfer supports aid in dying and has provided his scholarly view of Oregon's law to individuals in his congregation and to the public. He shared his religious perspective with me.

RABBI JOSHUA STAMPFER

One of the basic reasons I am so supportive and sympathetic to Oregon's law and to the whole program of aid in dying is because human beings have a profound need to be open and honest about themselves. They do not want to live the life of a lie. And generally, Oregon's law allows people who are dying the opportunity to do what they really believe is best for them. Without legal aid in dying people must live under a subterfuge, which I think is just wrong.

It is bad enough in our normal everyday lives that we learn for our own sake and for other people's sake not to be completely honest. We recognize it is not a very good thing in a society to be completely honest. Even our Jewish tradition tells us that to improve human relations, it's permissible to lie. Otherwise, you can tell the truth and hurt people's feelings and destroy relationships. That is difficult enough under normal circumstances, but when we're talking about the basic issues of life and death, it should not be a time for concealing the truth, and feeling as though you are in violation of laws or society if you choose to die. With the Oregon law, dying people in this state can do what they believe is right for them, be honest about it, and not carry the burden that they are breaking the law.

I cannot believe that any minister who regularly counsels patients in a hospital doesn't come to the conclusion that those patients have the right to end their suffering. I cannot count the number of times that people—many of them religious and pious—near the end of their lives and in tremendous suffering have asked me, "Why doesn't God take me? What possible use is it to God or to mankind for me to continue in this state?" I would think that every minister, rabbi or spiritual counselor who deals with dying patients would have the same experience.

No doubt there are times when patients' pleas to God for death are irrational. However, to assume these pleas are always irrational because other people believe physician aid in dying violates what they consider to be a basic spiritual principle is very wrong. Time and time again I hear from people who are clearly suffering, and who see no good purpose in continuing to suffer for as long as their dying takes.

Judaism places enormous emphasis on the preservation of life. Our Bible contains several times the phrase "choose life." The Bible stresses that you should choose life and that you can violate practically every commandment—certainly every ritual commandment—to preserve life. The only commandments you cannot violate to preserve life are those that impinge on somebody else's life. For example, you cannot take someone else's life to preserve your own life.

When a family from the Jewish tradition faces the request of a family member who wants to use aid in dying, I can understand very readily how they would feel, especially with a life that is so precious to them. Yet, that is the remarkable thing for which families have to be given the utmost credit—to be able to accept a family member's decision and not to reject it as an irrational decision. Instead, it is a full expression of love. Love is not necessarily the prolonging of life. Love can be expressed in other ways.

A dying person deciding whether or not to use aid in dying faces an enormously difficult decision for a whole string of reasons and even in the most understanding of families. One of the main considerations is the impact this decision is going to have on one's family. It requires a very loving and a very understanding family to agree to respect the person's wishes and to participate. There are good people who are simply emotionally limited and cannot give that level of unconditional love. To support this kind of end-of-life decision shows a remarkable understanding. To really love means that you really try to feel what the other person is feeling. You're not putting up a front. You're not fulfilling a duty. So I think a family that learns to accept this decision is one that is demonstrating profound love and empathy.

I publicly supported Oregon's Death with Dignity Act during both political campaigns and continue to do so with my congregation. In my career I have taken positions that were controversial, but I have never faced any organized resistance from the congregation. I remember when I introduced equality for women, I just did it. I had women participate in ways they never had before in the synagogue, and there were individuals who objected, but never in an organized way. The objections I got from individuals regarding aid in dying were, "How do you square this with Judaism's emphasis on life?" Or, "How do you square this with the notion that you are playing God?

That you are making decisions that only God should make? God gives life and therefore God takes life."

I answer them out of Jewish tradition—out of my view of Jewish tradition. I point out that my view is that God and man are partners. There is a strong Jewish tradition in which Jews compare God to a milking cow. Just as the calf needs the mother's milk, so the mother has to provide that milk. In turn, the cow needs to be relieved of the milk. So, just as we pray to God for everything, God needs our prayers. God wouldn't be God without our prayers. So there is a mutuality about our relationship with God. Therefore, as partners with God, we have the right to say to God, "We are grateful for the life you gave us, but that's enough."

God needs from us our worship, our adoration, our understanding. But when you are partners, then you have rights. We are not totally at God's disposal. One of the famous figures in modern Jewish history, Rabbi Levi Yitzchak of Berdichev, wrote a wonderful poem in which he sued God. He said, "God, you're our God, you're supposed to be protecting the Jewish people. Look what's happening to us. Why aren't you fulfilling your part of the covenant?" So there is, again, another challenge. It is not the only challenge, but it is a line of tradition in Judaism that says we have the right to challenge God.

So when a person exercises that right to end life under those clearly defined circumstances, he is fulfilling the duty of challenging God. It does not mean we are not grateful for our lives. I am grateful to God, but the time has come when that gift is no longer meaningful.

Life is God's gift, but all gifts carry with them—whether explicitly or implicitly—certain obligations. I spent six years on the Oregon Government Ethics Commission. Mostly what we dealt with were gifts. Lawmakers were receiving gifts, but they are not allowed to receive gifts, because every gift implicitly carries an obligation. So life is a gift and there are associated obligations. We have to do the best we can with our life. We did not merit our life. We did not earn it. We were given life. The obligation is to do with it the best that we can. But then when there comes a point when that no longer applies, then we have this right to participate in the end of our lives.

Throughout our history, Jews have challenged God, and for good reason. We have a strong tradition of not accepting dogma. Judaism does not have a church that issues dogma. So I think it is easier for Jews to adopt this position of end-of-life choices today because it is, in a sense, a challenge.

I have counseled a number of people who seriously entertained aid in dying and wanted to understand the religious implications of their act. I think on the whole, they are very grateful for a better understanding of how one can be an observant and believing Jew, and still go through with a physician-assisted death.

Victor Frankel came out of the Holocaust with the understanding that life has to have meaning to continue, and that it is possible to find meaning even in the Holocaust, even in the camps. Frankel's argument is very compelling. If you find meaning, if there is hope, if there is purpose, if there is sense, you have got to keep going, no matter how terrible it is.

However, individuals who choose to use the law to end their lives reach that decision when there is no purpose and no hope. And it varies with different people. Most people will cling to hope until their last breath. Some decide differently. What is most important from my perspective is for people to know they have a choice, and to enable them to make the best end-of-life decisions for themselves and for their loved ones.

REVEREND DR. PATRICIA ROSS

*R*everend Patricia Ross is a United Church of Christ minister in Portland, Oregon. She graduated from the Chicago Theological Seminary in 1966 with a Masters of Religious Education degree. She was ordained in 1982 after graduating from San Francisco Theological Seminary, and received her Doctor of Ministry from Chicago Theological Seminary in 2001. Reverend Ross has publicly supported legal aid in dying since the 1994 ballot measure. She has counseled dying congregants as well as other individuals regarding the theological aspects of using Oregon's assisted dying law. She notes, "My best strategy in preaching about death is to tell stories."

In October 2000 a young woman dying from a brain tumor sought my counsel regarding spiritual concerns because she wanted to use physician-assisted death. Dawn had excruciating pain as well as diminishing functions, and her life was adversely affected in many ways. She had always belonged to a religiously conservative church—a small, close knit community that was like an extended family to her. When Dawn got seriously ill, she really wanted to be able to end her life while she had some dignity and while she had some sense of who she was.

When Dawn expressed her concerns to her pastor, he told her that if she went through with it she would be condemned to hell. She said her minister directed the members of the church not to have anything to do with her until she changed her mind and agreed to die according to God's plan. According to Dawn, he warned them that "to continue in relationship with her while she contemplated this sinful act would put their souls in jeopardy as well." Her circle of support nearly vanished, and by the time I talked to her Dawn had only the people with whom she was staying and her boyfriend to comfort and support her.

I talked with her about a loving God who wants people to be able to live and to have some joy and to have a real life. And yes, suffering is a part of life, but it's not a requirement that we suffer interminably. Dawn just asked me plain and simple, "Do you think if I get the medication to die and then take it, will I be condemned to hell?" I told her, "No, that is not the kind of God I could have any faith in." We talked for quite a long time about various passages in the Bible because Dawn was a very biblically literate person. In particular, we discussed Ecclesiastes, Chapter 3, Verse 2: "There is a time to be born and a time to die." But the bottom line I kept coming back to was, "God is a loving God. God wants the best for all of God's children, and God does not want us to suffer interminably."

At the time I met with Dawn, I didn't know she had made a pact with her boyfriend regarding her death. She decided that if she couldn't take the medication to die, fearful that she would go to hell, she had a backup plan. She wanted her boyfriend to push her off the Vista Bridge in Portland because she knew he didn't believe that people went to hell, so she thought he would be okay, and ultimately, she would be innocent because she did not technically end her own life. I don't know if Dawn had thought about what that would do to him! If he loved her enough, I guess that he was willing to do that. And that kind of determination and that kind of focus just shows how much this law is needed—that a person would go to that length to end his or her life.

Not until after I had met with Dawn and I was talking about her situation with the referring Compassion caseworker did I learn about her desperate plan to jump off the bridge. The caseworker did tell me that Dawn thought our meeting had been helpful and so I was glad for that.

There is a belief among many Christians that there is something cleansing or strengthening or ennobling about suffering, or what I call redemptive suffering. Many saints and others have written about that and talked about the spiritual value of redemptive suffering. There are times when people have suffered through some horrendous things and really gained some insight. But when you are talking about end-of-life suffering, in my mind there comes a point when the suffering blots out any learning or any insight or any growth that might happen on a lesser level of suffering.

I believe there are times when we go through a horrible experience and we come out the other side and we say, "Well I sure wouldn't like to do that again but I did grow in this or I did learn something." But at the end of life there are circumstances where the pain is so great or when machines may be keeping some people going, and the body just isn't ready to let go, but everything else is shutting down, that I don't see the theological benefit of prolonging the suffering,

There is not a specific passage of scripture in the Bible that says assisted dying is okay, but there are many passages of scripture that call for mercy and love and justice and compassion. So I would look at those passages of scripture and help people think about those passages in terms of what their loved one is dealing with.

I do like the biblical passage, "There is a time to be born and a time to die." However, we have to see this in the context of the world as it is today. So much has changed. There are so many ways that life can be prolonged beyond what seems to be benefiting the person, that I think we do not respect that there is a time to live and a time to die in our practices.

We talk about the Commandment "Thou shalt not kill," and yet many people who say that still feel it is a right to have capital punishment, it is all right to go to war, and many people are killed. So most of those things are not lived out exactly as they are written from the Bible. One of the interpretations that I have really come to like is the idea that the Ten Commandments were not meant so much to be "thou shalt not" as much as to be a vision of the ideal. The Commandments offer a vision of a place and time where we would not need to have killing as an option; where relationships would be honored and respected so we would not be worried about adultery; and where people would have enough in their lives so that stealing and coveting would not be such a temptation. I see the Ten Commandments as more of a positive vision for what can be rather than just negative rules that you can't live up to.

Jesus said wonderful things about life and the meaning of life: "I come that you might have life and have it abundantly." And again, when you get to the point where you cannot do anything and you are in constant pain, when your body is just not responding to you in any way, that is not abundant life anymore.

I counseled one man with AIDS whom I had known for quite awhile—Bob was a friend of my daughter's. He had gotten the prescription to end his life. Bob was not a religious person but he did have concerns about whether using assisted dying would mean that he would be consigned to some punishment after death or some kind of terrible afterlife.

When I saw Bob he said he was very tired and ready to die but that he was afraid God would punish him for using physician-assisted dying. He said he just wanted some peace, some rest, but he wasn't sure death would be like that. Even though intellectually he rejected visions of fire and torture for the damned, those images haunted his thoughts as he prepared to use the prescribed medication. I told him that my understanding of God is that God is a loving friend who wants the best for each human being. I told him I believed God was waiting to hold him in love and to welcome him home.

Bob also asked me if I thought suffering was required in order to cleanse the soul. I told him I did not believe that God required suffering as a means of atonement but that God suffers with us and longs with us for the suffering to end. Bob told me he wasn't sure whether or not he would use the medication to die but it was very comforting to know he could do so.

Bob asked me if I would do a memorial service for him after he died. He wanted it to be positive and short. He wanted good music and for friends to share thoughts and memories. I said I would be glad to help plan such a service. A few days later his caregiver and former partner, Jim, who had returned to Portland to care for Bob in his final months, called to say that Bob had died naturally. We had a beautiful service for him at church, which was followed by a wonderful reception at the home Jim and Bob had shared for many years.

Bob's story really answers the question about people's fear of death. Some people seem to fear that when they die they will be punished. They don't want to believe this but it is a thought that seems hard for some people to dismiss. So when they are tired, sick, and ready to let go and die, one thing that holds them back is this fear that instead of the peaceful rest they long for their fate will be one of continued pain. I do not teach this in my church—nor do I know many who do—but some people's final images of Dante's *Inferno* are hard to dismiss. In my experience, it is not the dying process they fear—it is anxiety about what may follow death.

People express a couple of common concerns when they are dying and considering physician assisted death. The possibility that they would not have control is something that is quite important to people. Pain is not always the major concern, but it is certainly a factor. I think the indignities that go with losing control of your muscles and your bodily functions are very hard for people to accept.

When people share these fears, my approach is to say, "God is love. A loving God who thought to design us so well would not consign us to torture or discomfort." I reassure them that God is trying to help us to grow and to be fulfilled and to be strong and to be loving. Death is another step in that journey.

People have a very strong will to live. It surprises people sometimes how much they want to go on living even when it seems there is not much for them to live for. They have something inside of them that isn't ready to let go. You could call this by a lot of different names—the will, the soul, the spirit, almost the personality in a sense. Whatever you call it, this is the spark that makes me, me—and you, you. There is something very precious and very divine about that. It's hard to just give up.

I believe that dying is a beautiful mystery. It is not something to be afraid of. It is one more step in the journey. I have been surprised at how there can be many gross and ugly things about death, but in the end, death itself is really quite beautiful, and very mysterious.

Physician-assisted dying provides terminally ill, mentally competent adults a choice. They get to decide the manner and the timing of their death when their suffering becomes unconscionable. They get to decide who will be with them when they die. They can be surrounded by family and friends, if that is what they want. I think it is a wonderful opportunity for people to have that choice. For most people, even knowing that they have the medicine and they don't choose to take it—that in itself speaks well for why end-of-life choice is a really important and wonderful thing to have available for people.

I know other people completely disagree with me and they think I am horrible for holding this belief. I have talked to congregants and clergy who disagree with me. A couple of summers ago, I was with a group of clergy in Chicago and there had just been something on the news about Oregon's Death with Dignity Act. A Lutheran minister said to me, "What do you know about that law out in Oregon?" And I said, "Well, it's a good law. I know a little bit about it." Then he responded, "I think that's the worst thing that could possibly happen. I think it's just horrible." So I tried to talk to him a little about the law, and some of the people I know and some of the cases I have been aware of. He softened a little but he didn't let go of the idea that it was horrible. His response was so visceral—I was trying to figure out what it was that made him so opposed to the idea.

Nobody has to use physician-assisted dying. Nobody is forced to use it. And yet this minister was so vehement in his opposition and condemning of such a law. With further conversation I think the minister might have opened more to the possibility. However, I've been on panels with Christian people who just would not recognize my faith, my theology, or barely my humanity because I took the stance in support of end-of-life choice. I have become a monster to them. United Church of Christ ministers have a variety of opinions on any subject but I think they are a little more open to at least the possibility than other Christian ministers. They are much more social-justice minded.

There have been harsh criticisms from opponents who say using assisted dying is playing God. In my opinion, it is hard to say this particular act is playing God because there are so many ways in the world today that human beings do play God. God created us, I believe, to be co-creators with God. God didn't just put us here to be little puppets. God made us in God's image so that we would do amazing things. As a result, human beings have done some amazingly good things, and unfortunately, some amazingly bad things. But we are created, in my belief, to be co-creators with God.

Many older people were brought up to believe God tells us when we are going to die, or God makes it so that we die. They believe that it is all in God's hands, it is God's will. But we are far beyond that belief with all the things we can do in today's world to keep people alive. One older lady told me her husband died of pneumonia. She said pneumonia is the old man's friend. Well, now we have antibiotics, respirators, and many medical possibilities that shoo that old man's friend right out the door. So I don't think we are playing God with a law that provides for assisted dying.

If it ever came to the point that we were encouraging people to take medication to die soon, then I would call that playing God. But when people have a choice to take this medication to end their life, and if they feel that is right, then I don't see that as playing God. The Oregon law has provided specific rules that make it very hard to abuse physician-assisted dying.

Compassion in Dying:
Empowering Patients, Helping Families

$\mathcal{M}$ ost of this book is about Oregon, where aid in dying is open and legal. But Compassion is a national organization. We work with clients in every state—and sometimes internationally. Quietly, responsibly, and discreetly we have offered our patients hope and choice for more than ten years. When asked, we willingly attended hastened deaths long before Oregon's law came on line, and we continue to do so throughout the nation, following Compassion's careful procedures and strict guidelines. Our unique perspective is that mentally competent, terminally ill adults deserve excellent end-of-life care, state-of-the-art pain treatment, and options to achieve a peaceful and humane death at a time of their own choosing. We advocate vigorously for all three in courtrooms, legislatures, and public dialogue across the nation. That is the public side of our advocacy.

The private side takes place at the bedsides, living rooms, and kitchen tables of our clients. Sometimes our staff and volunteers respond urgently to a crisis; sometimes they support a family through many months of illness and decline. We offer our services without charge of any kind, to anyone who needs them. Thousands of generous supporters make our work possible with their charitable contributions.

Helen Beum is an advanced practice nurse who directs Compassion's Clinical Services nationally and supervises our volunteers. She compiled the following cases to illustrate the scope and effectiveness of Compassion's bedside advocacy.

Advance directives are often ignored. Compassion's advocates enforce these documents when clients cannot speak for themselves.
Case example

When one woman, a demented nursing home resident, stopped eating her doctor wanted to insert a feeding tube. Her only living relative, a niece, called Compassion for help. She knew her aunt would not want to prolong her life—she was eighty-seven and had been in the nursing home for several years. The niece knew her aunt had an advance directive but she was unable to advocate for her aunt from her home across the country.

A local Compassion volunteer visited the nursing home on the niece's behalf and spoke with the staff. A Compassion physician called the patient's physician and reminded him the patient had expressed a written desire not to have artificial nutrition. The tube was not inserted and the volunteer stayed in close touch with the patient and the niece. The Compassion volunteer made repeated visits to the nursing home to confirm the patient was comfortable. The woman died peacefully several weeks later.

Physicians may be reluctant to make a hospice referral. We advocate for early hospice care to get clients the support they need.
Case example

A patient with cancer and no close family was interested in learning how she might hasten death if her suffering became intolerable. When she contacted Compassion we asked her to consider enrolling in hospice. It was clear she needed hospice services and probably qualified for them. When she asked her physician about hospice, he told her she was not ready and refused to make a referral.

With the patient's permission, we contacted a local hospice and talked with staff about the patient's situation. They suggested the patient contact them and they would call the physician. If he still refused hospice, the patient could contact the hospice medical director. These conversations prompted the physician to make the referral and the patient received hospice care at home. She still wanted the option to hasten her death, but she received excellent pain and symptom management in the meantime.

Pain treatment is often woefully inadequate. We advocate for patients in pain.
Case example

A ninety-nine-year-old woman residing in a nursing home had increasing pain due to advanced osteoporosis and frequent fractures. Her son, a retired social worker and tireless advocate for his mother, contacted Compassion because he felt his mother was not getting proper treatment for her pain. The patient had been on the same dose of pain medication (a Duragesic patch—25 mcg strength) for over a year. The son had spoken with the staff of the nursing home and with the physician. Still nothing was done. We suggested he keep a record of his mother's pain. We also wrote him a letter suggesting that since patients develop a tolerance to opioids over time, the best course of action might be to increase the strength of the Duragesic patch to 50 mcg. He took this letter and his mother's pain record to her primary physician, who then faxed an order for the stronger patch to the nursing home within two hours. The son called back to say that his mother was much more comfortable on the stronger medication. He believes it was Compassion's reputation for effective legal advocacy that made the difference.

Stopping medical treatment can often bring a peaceful, humane death. We advocate for patients who wish to take this simple, legal step.
Case example

A man with a severe, progressive neuromuscular disease and diabetes decided he wanted to be allowed to die. He lived in a nursing home where the staff refused to even discuss his options. He contacted Compassion via email because he had difficulty talking on the phone. We gave him information about his legal right to stop medical treatment. With his permission we contacted the director of his nursing home and the Long Term Care Ombudsmen for that region. The patient willingly underwent a psychiatric evaluation and signed a disclaimer to protect the nursing home from legal action.

With these in place everyone finally agreed to honor his wishes. We helped the patient tell his aging father about his plans, contact a mortuary, and complete his will and other documents. A Compassion volunteer was at the bedside when the patient stopped his insulin and ceased taking any food and fluids. The volunteer stayed with him until he died peacefully two days later.

Doctors often confuse a rational wish to hasten death with irrational "suicide." We advocate for patients threatened with psychiatric commitment.

Case example

The daughter of a man dying of pancreatic cancer contacted Compassion immediately after her father was urgently hospitalized. Her sister had found him after he tried to die by taking several pain pills and putting a plastic bag over his head. In a panic, the sister had called 911. The doctors told the patient they were going to admit him to the psychiatric ward because he had become a danger to himself. His family was outraged. A Compassion psychiatrist immediately visited the patient in the hospital and spoke with his physician. Their conversation resulted in the understanding that the patient needed to go home to receive hospice care, not to the psychiatric ward for involuntary commitment. The patient went home three days after his daughter's call to Compassion and received excellent pain care from his hospice caregivers.

Patients without family caregivers are especially vulnerable. We advocate for patients who have no family support.
Case example

A patient with advanced breast cancer contacted Compassion because she wished information about hastening death. In visits to her home, the Compassion volunteer became concerned that the patient would soon be unable to care for herself. She had lived alone for years and had no close family. The patient agreed she would need more help soon. At the patient's request, the volunteer contacted a local in-patient hospice and took the patient for a tour. The patient agreed to move to the facility, where she received excellent care and support until she died.

Desperate patients contemplate desperate measures. Compassion's advocacy prevents violent suicide.
Case example

A man with neck cancer contacted Compassion after he returned home from a doctor's appointment. The physician had told the patient chemotherapy was no longer working and his tumor would soon invade the artery in his neck. The doctor explained, "When that happens, you will bleed to death." The patient, a policeman and avid hunter, owned several guns. He carried one with him wherever he went. Later, when talking with a Compassion volunteer, he asked, "Tell me why I shouldn't shoot myself right now?" The volunteer talked with him about the troubling memories a violent death would leave his family. She recommended hospice care, and explained other options. They discussed how the patient might obtain medication from his physician to hasten his death peacefully. His volunteer stayed in close touch.

With hospice care the patient had several good months. He planned to move eventually to a nursing home so his young son would not see him weak and "out of it." One day in November, the patient told his Compassion volunteer, "I wish I were dead.

If I could get to my guns, I would do it here and now." The volunteer immediately called in a medical advisor, who spoke with the patient, his wife, and then his physician, to make recommendations for a stronger pain medication.

A short time later the volunteer visited the patient and learned he was ready to obtain medication to hasten his death. Once he knew this process was moving forward and he would soon have the means to a peaceful and dignified death, the patient relaxed. He stopped talking about shooting himself. He did obtain the medication but died without taking it, in his own bed a month later with his wife and son beside him. His wife told Compassion, "I was really sure he was going to shoot himself until you came along. He knew there was another way and that made all the difference."

Terminal illness places tremendous stress on relationships. Our advocacy promotes effective communication between patients and family members.
Case example

The daughter of a man with advanced throat cancer contacted Compassion because her father asked her to investigate his options. She had never experienced the death of a loved one and did not really understand what to expect as her father weakened and was dying. He did not talk with his daughter much about his concerns. We described some decisions her father would soon have to make, suggested hospice and better pain care, and sent a packet of materials to the daughter.

The daughter reported later that she read Compassion's booklet, "A Gentle Death," out loud to her father and mother. They had a profound and moving talk and connected in a way they never had before. Everyone cried and held each other and the doors of communication opened. Her father died two weeks later at home with the support of hospice. The family felt Compassion gave them the tools to talk honestly and share their feelings with one another.

Eligibility for Oregon's Law

To be eligible to receive a prescription for medication to hasten death, a patient must be:

- An adult resident of Oregon;
- Capable (able to make and communicate health care decisions); and
- Diagnosed with a terminal illness, likely to result in death within 6 months.

Eligible patients undergo a thorough screening and application process:

- The patient makes three requests, two oral and one written;
- Two individuals witness the written request and one witness may be neither a family member, heir or health care provider;
- The physician explains the patient's diagnosis and prognosis and offers hospice care, pain control and other comfort care;
- A second physician confirms the diagnosis and prognosis and that the request is voluntary, enduring and not prompted by impaired judgment.
- If either physician suspects psychological impairment the patient is referred for evaluation and counseling by a psychologist or psychiatrist;
- Fifteen days separate the first request and the writing of a prescription. Forty-eight hours separate the written request and the writing of the prescription;
- The physician must ask the patient to notify next-of-kin and reinforce that the request may be rescinded at any time;
- Both physicians and the pharmacist who fills the prescription submit detailed reports to the Oregon Department of Human Services.

For more information on Oregon's law:
www.compassionindying.org

Timeline of Legal Aid in Dying

1987, 1989, 1991 Oregon State Senator Frank Roberts sponsors legislation granting individuals options for the end of life. None ever leaves committee.

April 1993 At the peak of the AIDS epidemic, eleven activists establish Compassion in Dying in Seattle, Washington and publicly declare their intention to counsel mentally competent, terminally ill patients on aid in dying. The organization publishes specific eligibility criteria, guidelines, and safeguards and volunteers to attend deaths, so clients who choose aid in dying do not have to die alone. Compassion's medical model of aid in dying begins to evolve with client assessment, professional referrals, an interdisciplinary team of volunteers and self-administered medication.

July 1993 Oregon Right to Die, Political Action Committee (PAC) is founded by Eli Stutsman, Peter Goodwin, Myriam Coppens, Margaret Grosswiler and Elven Sinnard in order to create and achieve passage of Oregon's Death with Dignity Act.

January 1994 Compassion in Dying files a legal challenge to Washington's ban on aid in dying in *Compassion et al v. Washington*. Compassion lawyers represent four physicians and three terminally ill patients in the case that later becomes known as *Washington v. Glucksberg*.

July 1994 Compassion's second constitutional challenge begins when three New York physicians and three terminally patients challenge that state's ban on aid in dying. The case name is *Quill et al v. Roppell* but later becomes known as *Vacco v. Quill*.

November 1994 Oregon voters approve Measure 16, the Oregon Death with Dignity Act, by 51 percent to 49 percent. Elven Sinnard (left), Peter Goodwin, M.D. (right), and Barbara Coombs Lee are chief petitioners.

December 1994 In response to a lawsuit *(Lee v. Oregon)* brought by the National Right to Life Committee, U.S. District Judge Michael Hogan enjoins Oregon's aid in dying law on the grounds that it endangers the plaintiffs, who oppose the new law. The injunction keeps aid in dying illegal in Oregon.

August 1995 Judge Hogan rules the Oregon Death with Dignity Act is unconstitutional because it discriminates against the terminally ill.

February 1996 Compassion in Dying publishes data of its first thirteen months experience in Washington State in an article titled "Observations Concerning Terminally Ill Patients Who Choose Suicide." The authors report that while many terminally ill patients request information, only a few take medication to hasten death.

March—April 1996 Appellate courts on opposite sides of the country rule in Compassion's lawsuits that the right of a terminally ill person to receive medication to hasten death is protected by the U.S. Constitution. An eleven-judge panel of the Ninth Circuit rules that absolute criminalization of aid in dying violates liberty and privacy protections. One month later the Second Circuit rules that banning aid in dying violates equal protection principles because people kept alive on machines can stop them to achieve a peaceful death but those with no machines have no recourse. The cases now known as *Washington v. Glucksberg* and *Vacco v. Quill* are on their way to the U.S. Supreme Court.

February 1997 The Ninth Circuit Court of Appeals reverses Judge Hogan's ruling, orders him to lift his injunction against the Oregon Death with Dignity Act and dismisses the lawsuit. Plaintiffs seek a review at the U.S. Supreme Court and the law remains in limbo.

June 1997 Under enormous pressure from Oregon Right to Life and Oregon Catholic Conference, Oregon's legislature forces a special election to repeal the Death with Dignity Act. No similar attempt to overturn the will of Oregon voters had occurred since 1908.

June 1997 The U.S. Supreme Court reverses both the Second Circuit and the Ninth Circuit in *Washington v. Glucksberg* and *Vacco v. Quill.* It finds state laws barring aid in dying are not unconstitutional and refers the issue to the political process within states. The Supreme Court concluded, "Throughout the Nation, Americans are engaged in an earnest and profound debate about the morality, legality and practicality of [physician aid in dying]. Our holding permits this debate to continue, as it should in a democratic society."

October 27, 1997 The U.S. Supreme Court having denied plaintiff's request for review of *Lee v. Oregon,* the U.S. District Court is forced to lift its injunction and The Death with Dignity Act finally becomes available to Oregonians.

November 1997 On election day voters defeat the repeal initiative by a relative landslide, 60 percent to 40 percent. The next day the Administrator of the

Federal Drug Enforcement Administration, with prodding from Congressman Henry Hyde and Senator Orrin Hatch, issues a letter stating Oregon's law violates the federal Controlled Substances Act. The administration announces the Department of Justice will determine whether this is a correct interpretation of the law. Ray Frank becomes the first person known to ask to use the law. After deciding he does not need to use his gun because he can use the law, Frank dies peacefully during the fifteen-day waiting period.

March 1998 Compassion's client "Helen" becomes the first known American to take medication legally to hasten death. After a twenty-two year battle with cancer, she dies peacefully surrounded by family.

June 1998 Attorney General Janet Reno issues her interpretation that the Controlled Substances Act does not authorize the federal government to act against doctors complying with Oregon law. The same day Congressman Henry Hyde introduces the Lethal Drug Abuse Prevention Act (LDAPA) to create a federal crime of intending to cause death with a controlled substance. U.S. Senator Don Nickles introduces an identical bill in the U.S. Senate. Medical and patient advocacy groups see the bill as a threat to pain care for the terminally ill. Despite predictions of easy passage, the bill never reaches a vote in either chamber.

February 1999 *The New England Journal of Medicine* publishes Oregon's first-year statistics on aid in dying. The data bring international media attention to the successful stewardship of the law. Twenty-four people received prescriptions under the law and sixteen used the medication to hasten death.

October 1999 U.S House of Representatives passes the Pain Relief Promotion Act (PRPA) by 271 to 156. Like LDAPA, Henry Hyde's new bill would nullify Oregon law and threaten pain care throughout the nation.

February 2000 Oregon officials report on the second year of aid in dying. Thirty-three people received prescriptions and twenty-seven died after taking the medication.

October 2000 After a courageous and diligent filibuster threat by Oregon Senator Ron Wyden the 106th Congress adjourns with the PRPA defeated and Oregon's law intact.

November 2000 Maine voters consider a referendum to adopt an Oregon-style aid in dying law and narrowly reject it, 51.5 percent to 48.5 percent.

February 2001 Oregon officials report on the third year of aid in dying. Thirty-nine people received prescriptions and twenty-seven died after taking the medication.

November 2001 On election day, shortly after 9/11, Attorney General John Ashcroft issues a Directive based on his opinion that the federal Controlled Substances Act authorizes him to prosecute doctors who prescribe medications for aid in dying in Oregon and elsewhere. If enforced, the Ashcroft Directive would overturn two statewide elections and nullify the votes of more than 650,000 Oregonians. Within forty-eight hours Compassion joins the state of Oregon in a legal challenge. In order to prevent irreversible harm to terminally ill Oregonians who depend on the choice of aid in dying, U.S. District Court Judge Robert E. Jones issues a restraining order, preventing the Ashcroft Directive from being enforced.

February 2002 Oregon officials issue the fourth-year report on aid in dying. In 2001 forty-four people received prescriptions and twenty-one used the medication to hasten their death.

April 2002 Judge Jones rules that Attorney General Ashcroft has no authority to intervene in the practice of medicine in Oregon. Oregon's Death with Dignity Act remains in place.

September 2002 John Ashcroft's Department of Justice appeals its loss to the U.S. Court of Appeals. Court filings include briefing from both sides and from a host of Amici Curiae (friends of the court) who submit arguments on their view of aid in dying in Oregon and the political process. Medical groups contend the Ashcroft Directive, like the failed congressional bills, would place physicians in an untenable position and deter pain treatment for dying patients.

February 2003 Oregon authorities release five years of data on the state's experience with aid in dying. A total of 198 patients have completed the process to obtain life-ending medication. Of those, 129 took medication to hasten their death. Approximately 150,000 Oregonian residents have died of all causes over this time.

May 2003 A three-judge panel of the Ninth Circuit Court of Appeals hears arguments from the state of Oregon, Compassion, and physicians and pharmacists on one side, and from Department of Justice lawyers on the other in *Oregon v. Ashcroft*. A ruling had not been issued at the time of this writing, August 2003.

About the Editor

Barbara Coombs Lee is President of Compassion in Dying Federation, a non-profit organization dedicated to improving the care and expanding the options available to the terminally ill. She practiced as a nurse and physician assistant for twenty years before beginning a career in law and health policy. Since then she has devoted her professional life to furthering individual choice and empowerment in health care.

As a private attorney, as staff to the Oregon State Senate, as a managed care executive and finally as a

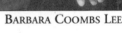

BARBARA COOMBS LEE

Chief Petitioner for Oregon's Death with Dignity Act, she has championed initiatives that enable individuals to consider a full range of choices and be full participants in their health care decisions.

Coombs Lee received her undergraduate and nursing educations at Vassar College and Cornell University. She obtained training in medicine at the University of Washington and a law degree from Northwestern School of Law, Lewis & Clark College. She is a member of the Oregon State Bar.

Coombs Lee is a frequent presenter before national and local professional organizations, churches and community forums. Her appearances also include international forums and broadcast media such as NBC News, 60 Minutes, McNeil Lehrer News Hour, NPR Morning Edition. She has testified several times before the U.S. Congress on end-of-life issues.

Coombs Lee lives and works in Portland, Oregon. This is her first book.

Other Books by NewSage Press

*N*ewSage Press publishes nonfiction books on a variety of topics. The following books address death and grief. For a complete list of our titles, including chapter excerpts, visit our web site: www.newsagepress.com

Death Without Denial, Grief Without Apology:
  A Guide for Facing Death and Loss
  Barbara K. Roberts

Common Heroes: Facing a Life Threatening Illness
  Eric Blau, M.D.

Life Touches Life: A Mother's Story of Stillbirth and Healing
  Lorraine Ash, Foreword by Christiane Northrup, M.D.
  Available April 2004

Blessing the Bridge: What Animals Teach Us
  About Death, Dying, and Beyond
  Rita Reynolds, Foreword by Gary Kowalski

Three Cats, Two Dogs, One Journey Through Multiple Pet Loss
  David Congalton

NewSage Press
PO Box 607, Troutdale, OR 97060-0607

Phone Toll Free 877-695-2211, Fax 503-695-5406
Email: info@newsagepress.com

Distributed to bookstores by Publishers Group West
800-788-3123, PGW Canada 800-463-3981